Financial Management Strategies for Arts Organizations

Financial Management Strategies for Arts Organizations

by Frederick J. Turk & Robert P. Gallo

Peat, Marwick, Mitchell & Co.
Avis Allman, Research Consultant

ACA Books
A Program of the American Council for the Arts
New York, New York

Copyright © 1984 American Council for the Arts

Edited by Bruce Peyton

Designed by T.H. Richards
Jacket design by Celine Brandes, Photo Plus Art

Typography by ILNY Communications and Media Corporation
Printing by Port City Press

Manager of Publishing: Robert Porter

Library of Congress Cataloging in Publication Data

Turk, Frederick J.
    Financial management strategies for arts organizations.
    1. Arts—United States—Finance.
    2.Arts—United States—Management.
      I. Gallo, Robert P.
      II. Title.
NX711.U5T8   1984   700'.68'1   84-12352

ISBN 0-915400-40-5

American Council for the Arts
570 Seventh Avenue
New York, New York 10018

*This publication was made possible by the generous
support of the following contributors:*

Peat, Marwick, Mitchell & Co.
Phillips Petroleum Foundation
Shell Companies Foundation

Contents

APPENDICES

Contents

List of Exhibits

Acknowledgements

WE WISH TO EXPRESS OUR APPRECIATION to several people who were important contributors as we developed this book. Without their interest, support, and most importantly, their efforts in providing quality service to nonprofit organizations, we would not have had the benefit of their extensive experience and the rich material they have produced.

First, we acknowledge the leadership of Charles A. Nelson, recently retired Principal at Peat Marwick. He was coauthor of *Financial Management for the Arts* and originated the Henrik Arts Association case which has been updated for this new book. His inspiration and continuing support as mentor and friend have been instrumental in completing this book.

Other colleagues, namely Herbert Folpe, Herbert Hansen, David G. Horner, Eva Klein, R. Schuyler Lesher, John McLaughlin, Bruce Nickerson, Dr. Alceste Pappas, and Daniel D. Robinson (retired partner), all provided invaluable resource material coming from their many writings and years of work at Peat Marwick. In particular, we should mention David G. Horner, whose article on strategic planning, published in Peat Marwick's *Management Focus* magazine, served as the basis for the material on pages 28–34 in Chapter 3. Further, Dr. Alceste Pappas' writings on organization were used in Chapter 5 to prepare the material on pages 61–66. The typing and related administrative support provided by Patricia Leddin throughout this effort is much appreciated by the authors.

Robert Porter of the ACA served as editor, leader, inspirationalist, and chief protagonist throughout this project. Without his continued and patient support, this book would never have been completed. His wisdom and sensitivity were important contributions to the treatment given to the many financial management matters presented. In addition, the editing skills provided by Bruce Peyton were of great value in helping us to shape the material and make it more easily understood.

Avis Allman served us in an exemplary fashion as consultant, conducting important research, updating the Henrik Arts Center case, and collecting and organizing much of the original material written by the Peat Marwick professionals mentioned.

The Peat Marwick partnership deserves special mention in this undertaking. Peat Marwick has graciously supported the authors and staff in preparing this book for the American Council for the Arts.

Finally, we would like to acknowledge our families—especially our respective partners, Rachel and Maureen. Without their patience and continuing support and encouragement, we would not have completed this project.

Although the authors appreciate the participation and support of many people, in the final analysis we accept full responsibility for the results of this effort.

Robert P. Gallo
Frederick J. Turk

Introduction

WE BELIEVE that the financial management process exists
to support the management process (planning and budgeting, organizing, controlling, and evaluating). Accordingly, it
is assumed that financial management should assist the governing board, the director, and the staff in carrying out their
fiduciary responsibilities in order to achieve organizational
mission, goals, and objectives.

This book describes generally accepted financial management principles and practices and illustrates them where
appropriate. The case study in Chapter 2, which serves as
the focus of illustrations used in subsequent chapters, is an
expansion of that presented in *Financial Management for the
Arts*. The revised illustration depicts a larger, more complex
arts organization while retaining elements applicable to
smaller organizations as well.

Chapter 3 focuses on strategic planning, the process of determining what should be done programmatically and what resources are necessary to present these programs to the public. Budgeting, Chapter 4, describes the process of assigning resources to carry out the plan. Budgets list sources of income and support and outline specifically how resources will be allocated. The emphasis in these two chapters is on the financial aspects of planning and budgeting.

Chapter 5 focuses on organization, the process of identifying roles and directing people to carry out activities according to plan.

Chapters 6, 7, 8, and 9 discuss the key elements in establishing an effective financial management process. Chapter 6 describes the financial management information system that should be in place to support decisionmaking and control over the use of resources. Chapter 7 explains the key financial accounting principles and practices applicable to arts organizations. Chapter 8 focuses on ratio analysis and management indicators which may be used to maintain optimum levels of performance. Chapter 9 describes the asset management practices that should be followed by arts organizations.

The appendix presents an overview of selected topics of increasing interest to arts organizations. These include data processing and federal grants accounting, reporting, and related compliance issues.

This book contains many subjects of growing concern to arts organizations. We recognize that almost all arts organizations—large or small—are faced with increasingly complex financial management issues. What is certain is that there is a need for more sophisticated management—particularly financial management—of arts organizations. This book is designed to help arts managers and governing boards with the many issues and decisions that they must make that will affect the future of their organizations.

1

Overview

IN THE LAST DECADE, Americans have enjoyed access to a wider variety of art forms than ever before, and they have taken advantage of that access in ever-increasing numbers. According to *Americans and the Arts*, a 1980 survey of public opinion conducted by the National Research Center of the Arts, Inc. for the American Council for the Arts, leisure time was shrinking during the latter half of the seventies, thereby increasing competition to attract people with limited time and money to spend. Yet, during the same period, arts attendance increased markedly; participation by people who play musical instruments, write creatively, dance, sing, sculpt, make pottery, paint, draw or work with theatre groups was on the rise; and public opinion regarding the importance of the arts in American life was overwhelmingly positive. Clearly, the arts have become an essential element in our diverse society.

Based on the public's increasing awareness and interest, the arts in America have grown at an unprecedented rate. This did not occur, however, in a topsy-turvy fashion. Rather, it has required much careful attention and personal sacrifice on the part of artists and others deeply committed to the arts. In particular, some arts organizations have seen the need to give special attention to the careful management of resources, including people, facilities, and most of all, money. The application of sound management practices has greatly helped those organizations trying to respond to the growing demands of Americans for more and better art and at least cost to the community at large.

Most recently, new economic conditions are causing hardships for many arts organizations, conditions which affect their ability to continue and to expand the fine work of the past. In recent years the inflationary spiral has caused costs to rise rapidly, while at the same time, government funding in real terms has been reduced. Although it has been assumed that private sector financing would increase to take up the slack, so far this has not happened—even though real increases in private sector giving have occurred in recent years. This is a good trend but certainly not sufficient to satisfy the money needs of the arts.

Arts organizations—like any enterprise—must be constantly vigilant of changing economic conditions, and they must be prepared to make adjustments in the way they conduct their affairs. Essentially, this means applying sound

EXHIBIT 1
The Management Process

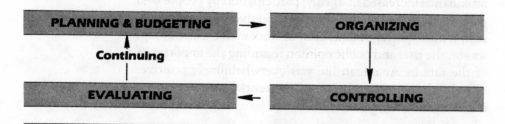

management principles in order to use precious resources most efficiently.

THE MANAGEMENT PROCESS

The management process is composed of four discrete activities:
1. **Planning and Budgeting**—the process of deciding what should be done and what resources are available to the arts organization;
2. **Organizing**—the process of authorizing and directing the use of resources to carry out programmatic activities according to the plan;
3. **Controlling**—the process of reviewing progress to determine how well the arts organization is doing and to identify changes that may be necessary to cope with circumstances that were unforseen when the plans were developed; and
4. **Evaluating**—the process of examining the results of programmatic activities to determine the extent to which plans and objectives were achieved and how they might be better conducted in the future.

As shown in Exhibit 1, the management process is continuing and cyclical. Once the activities of planning and budgeting, organizing, controlling, and evaluating are completed, the process begins again with planning.

MAJOR RESOURCES IMPLICIT IN THE MANAGEMENT PROCESS

As shown in Exhibit 2, there are important relationships among resources in the management process. An arts organization's resources are combined to produce programs for audiences. Throughout the management process, the organization is concerned with using and directing its resources

EXHIBIT 2
Relationship of Resources

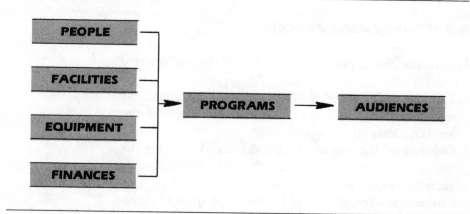

most effectively. A brief description of each resource category follows.

1. **People**—the artists, the governing board, the director, professional staff, support staff, and others who are available to conduct or support programs. In addition, an important resource for many arts organizations is volunteers who supplement the staff in conducting programs.
2. **Facilities**—galleries, theatres, offices, and other physical facilities.
3. **Equipment**—furniture, office equipment, vehicles, instruments, scenery, costumes, props, sound systems, and the like.
4. **Finances**—funds available to pay for staff, equipment, and facilities. Organizational funds are primarily received from gifts and grants, memberships, investment income, admissions, tuition revenue, government appropriations, and auxiliary activities, such as concessions.

These resources are combined and adjusted as necessary to produce programs, the services provided by arts organizations. They may be PRIMARY PROGRAMS designed to fulfill an organization's purpose as specified in its charter and bylaws, or SUPPORT PROGRAMS, which exist to help carry out primary programs. Primary programs should coincide with an organization's mission, goals, and objectives. For example, in a museum such programs might be curatorial and conservation, exhibits, education, fellowships, and public information. Support programs would include membership maintenance, fundraising, and administrative support.

AUDIENCES, the recipients of program services, are a primary reason for the existence of the arts organization. If a receptive audience does not exist, one could argue that the organization has neither purpose nor mission and should not continue into the future.

The combination of organizational resources to produce programs for receptive audiences is the ultimate challenge of the management process. One can visualize a large television screen with multiple dials. As audience demands and environmental conditions change, these dials, representing institutional resources, must be adjusted to keep the picture in focus. The management process involves using these dials (i.e., resources) effectively and efficiently to accomplish the mission, goals, and objectives of the arts organization.

THE FINANCIAL MANAGEMENT PROCESS

The three primary functions that make up the financial management process are financial management, financial accounting, and compliance assurance. Within the overall management process, these functions support the activities associated with planning and budgeting, organizing, controlling, and evaluating. Financial management does so by measuring, analyzing, and interpreting the financial effect of resource decisions, both historically and prospectively. Financial accounting involves recording, classifying, and summarizing transactions and events which are of a financial character. In compliance assurance, policies and procedures are established to ensure that legal restrictions, regulations, and rules imposed by third party authorities are followed. These authorities include the federal government, the state government, and the public.

KEY ELEMENTS IN THE FINANCIAL MANAGEMENT PROCESS

Effective financial management comprises the following elements:

1. A clearly defined organizational structure with all financially related responsibilities and authorities assigned;
2. Financial policies established by the governing board and the director which conform to those suggested for arts organizations in authoritative literature;
3. A financial management information system that operates effectively and produces accurate and timely information which satisfies the needs of the governing board, the director, and the staff; and
4. A detailed definition of the financial activities associated with measuring, analyzing, and interpreting the effect of resource decisions—prospectively and historically.

This combination of organization structure, policies, an information system, and detailed definition of activities must operate in equilibrium if resources are to be used effectively and efficiently to accomplish an organization's mission, goals, and objectives. The key ingredients of each must be understood and applied by managers and trustees. The chapters that follow describe the major ingredients applicable to each element of the financial management process. It is up to managers and trustees to adapt these ingredients to the peculiarities of their organizations to derive the best model to satisfy their needs.

2

The Financial Management Dilemma—A Case Study

THE HENRIK CASE STUDY presented here is a description of an arts center comprising a museum, a ballet company, an education division, and other related arts entities. The Henrik Arts Center is referred to throughout this book to help the reader understand and visualize some of the financial management concepts being presented.

EARLY HISTORY OF HENRIK

The Henrik Art Association was created in 1947 to receive the gift of a Hudson River mansion from the family of Joseph Van Felder, from whose apple orchards and land speculations the family fortune had been derived. The mansion housed the Van Felder Gallery as well as the offices of the Association.

For the first seventeen years, the Gallery was the focus of all Association efforts. Although two or three good Hudson River paintings came with the house and a fine Giacometti sculpture was donated by a Van Felder daughter in 1960, the collection as a whole was, by 1964, still quite undistinguished and completely lacking in artistic unity. Assembled largely by a volunteer committee, the material included paintings (most of them rather poor) by local artists, some good reproductions of masterpieces, a few excellent original works of various periods, and even a collection of Waterford crystal and some fine old silver.

In 1965, the Association hired its first professional director, Gregory James, who proved to be an ideal choice. Under his leadership, a range of programs was developed which resulted in increased membership contributions and grants. His chief successes were the rotating exhibitions of first-class shows from major museums; a booming art instruction program in painting, ceramics, and sculpture for both adults and young people; and an art appreciation program for children co-sponsored by the public schools and held in the Gallery. Also, each year a Van Felder Exhibit was held at which original works were displayed and cash prizes were awarded; an admission fee was charged for the event. During James' ten years as director of the Henrik Arts Association, membership increased from 600 to 1,750, several foundation grants were obtained, and public funds were provided for the school program.

In 1975, James accepted the position of education director at a major museum in New York City, just over 100 miles to the south. Even before his departure, signs were appearing of a leveling off of activity—memberships had remained static for two years, and there had been a slight decline in the patron gift category. Nevertheless, James' successor, Fred Potter, was an imaginative, energetic young man with many ideas for moving the association forward again.

Potter developed a noteworthy permanent collection (without giving up the traveling exhibits). The best of contemporary crafts—weaving, pottery, metalworking, macramé, sculptured furniture, etc.—were assembled and given a first-class regional showcase, creating for the first time a significant independent reputation for the Van Felder Gallery. Potter pointed out that some of the best craftsmen in their respective fields were associated with the gallery as either instructors or students, which was a natural and historical basis for the collection.

HENRIK CRAFTS COUNCIL

In order to create an active leadership relationship with the local crafts community, Potter established the Henrik Crafts Council. The organization's activities were designed for craftspeople, craft historians, and craft lovers of all ages. Programs would feature renowned guest craftspeople; other activities would include workshops in ceramics and weaving and special mini-workshops for children. Members of the council would be given the opportunity to exhibit in the annual Van Felder Crafts Exhibit. Guest jurors would be invited each year for this major regional show.

EDUCATION

Potter and the board decided that a more concentrated focus and organization was needed in the educational program, which had always served as a minor side arm of the exhibition program. To this end, a separate department was created comprising three major programs: Educational Services, the Henrik School of the Arts, and Volunteer Programs.

The Educational Services Program extended into the public schools and local communities. Programs by professionals provided educational arts involvement though lecture-demonstrations, classroom visits, student and teacher workshops, PTA and community group presentations and workshops, exhibits, films, and slide programs. Thirty-five traveling exhibits packaged in large cases, trunks, and boxes were made available for classroom use as supplemental teaching aids on a two-week rental basis. Exhibits were designed so that many artifacts could be handled and used by the students or community groups, with the content being emphasized through well-researched labels and teacher guides. Special art programs for teachers, administrators, and PTA groups were also a major function of the expanded Educational Services.

The Henrik School of the Arts consisted of two major components: Art Instruction for Adults and the Young People's Art Center. Adult classes were offered in painting, drawing, watercolor, mixed media, sculpture, and a variety of fiber arts and ceramics. Each class met once a week for three hours; levels ranging from beginning through intermediate and advanced professional artist-teachers were utilized for all instruction. The Young People's Art Center was open to young people from the ages of six to eighteen. Designed to extend the opportunity of art training beyond that normally received in school, the art school exposed students to work in a variety of media by allowing them to work with professional artists, craftspeople, and teachers.

The staff of the Volunteer Programs consisted of docents and museum aides. More than forty professionally-trained docents were recruited to guide groups of school children and adults through the center, discussing both permanent collections and changing exhibitions. After an eight-week introductory course, these volunteer guides attended a series of in-depth lectures and seminars. After one year of training, the docents were prepared to conduct their first tours of the center. However, training never stopped; classes, briefings and workshops were held periodically.

BALLET

During the years prior to Potter's appointment, a local performing group called the Hudson River Ballet Company had
been developing rapidly. Started in 1970 by a few dance
students from a neighboring college, the company began performing a repertory ranging from classical to contemporary.
In 1976, the company was awarded its first state arts agency
grant, which allowed the group to tour regionally. It received
wide critical acclaim, and this encouraged performers from
out-of-town, nationally-known, professional companies to
join the performances.

In late 1976, the ballet company approached the board of
the Henrik Arts Association concerning a joint venture.
The ballet company needed a permanent home in which to
perform and to establish a ballet school. Their recent, successful tour had demonstrated the need for an active performing arts program in the region. In return for a permanent home, the ballet company would perform twice a year
and conduct outreach programs into the local school
systems. Additionally, they would sponsor a dance film
festival each year to encourage interest in the discipline and
expand the students' knowledge of the world of dance. Finally, a classical ballet school would be established to offer daily
training at all levels of development. Guided by a proposed
staff of two full-time and five part-time instructors, classes
would include pre-ballet for children, mime and stage move-
ment for actors, and adult ballet classes designed for maximum convenience for those with busy schedules. The
Henrik School of Ballet would function as the home of the
Hudson River Ballet Company, whose dancers would be
drawn from among both students and faculty, with classes
and rehearsals held daily. Operation of the school was planned
to begin in 1982.

Upon consideration, the Henrik Association Board of
Directors adopted a resolution in early 1977 to expand their
mission to include performing arts. A capital campaign

would be initiated to build a facility to house the Hudson River Ballet Company and book out-of-town theater, music, and dance programs.

HENRIK ARTS CENTER

In order to indicate its new direction and scope of programs, the board changed the organization's name from Henrik Arts Association to Henrik Arts Center. In 1977, the board officially initiated a capital campaign for building improvement and expansion. Through the use of an outside professional fundraising firm located in New York City, the association, over a period of three years, raised $1.8 million. In 1978, the campaign was significantly assisted by a major $250,000 National Endowment for the Arts' Challenge Grant, which was supported by the governor and local politicians. Major funds of $500,000 were donated by Computer Chips Inc., a Fortune 100 corporation which had moved its world headquarters to the area just two years prior. Computer Chips, Inc. needed a rich local cultural environment in order to persuade prospective staff and their families to move into the region. Remaining funds were received from a few regional foundations, local businesses, state funds, and a massive united appeal to the community.

In 1979, construction began on the first performing arts facility for the area—a 296-seat, 5,500-square-foot, multi-purpose, full-stage proscenium theatre. It was equipped with a twenty-dimmer lighting system, an inventory of over one hundred lighting instruments, and an extensive audio facility capable of being augmented by an in-house reinforcement/amplification system. Topping off the theater's audio-visual inventory were four sixteen-millimeter film projectors.

The stage floor was covered with a surface specifically designed for dance, while overhead a counterweight fly system extended all the way from the main curtain to the back wall. This system was designed to accommodate back-drops and other large pieces of scenery, as well as maskings for redefining the performing space. Thereby, the theater was flexible enough to function as an intimate performance space for both full-stage theatrical productions and lecture/demostrations.

Additionally, major improvements were made in the museum exhibition space and storage areas to ensure proper temperature and humidity controls. These changes allowed better care of the collections and increased flexibility in the types of traveling exhibitions.

Finally, a 413-square-foot museum shop was established to extend the impact of the collections and exhibitions of Henrik Arts Center. The shop also provided a mechanism to increase and diversify income sources.

The performing space was completed in September 1980 and was occupied in November 1981. During the most recent season, the Hudson River Ballet Company performed a spring concert series of six performances, *The Nutcracker* was produced eleven times, and outside bookings included one performance by a major regional theater, two organ concerts, a five-part film series, and a Christmas film series. To date, the facility has had full houses, and the performing arts program has been well received by the press and the local community.

The Museum Shop also began operation in the late 1970s. In broad categories, the shop inventory covered historical materials and artifacts, arts and crafts from the region, and the latest educational toys. Books, art post cards, and reproductions focusing on the arts and crafts and ballet were secured from the best presses across the nation.

THE BUDGET

Fred Potter, after all that he has accomplished, had decided to accept a new position as director of a major museum in

EXHIBIT 3
Henrik Arts Center Statement of Activity (Actual)
Fiscal Year Ended 6/30/84

Revenues	Total	%
Earned		
Shops	$ 80,765	4.8
Tuition/Class Fees	37,883	2.2
Admission/Ticket Sales	136,646	8.0
Fees/Commissions	17,620	1.0
Trips/Workshops	10,881	0.6
Endowment	178,408	10.5
Other Income	19,382	1.1
Total Earned	481,585	28.2
Grants		
City	33,478	2.0
County	100,433	5.9
State	66,955	3.9
Federal	113,648	6.7
Private	25,549	1.5
Total Grants	340,063	20.0
Contributions		
Individuals—Annual Giving	195,587	11.5
Corporations/Foundations	650,000	38.2
Memberships	35,233	2.1
Total Contributions	880,820	51.8
Total Revenues	$ 1,702,468	100.0

EXHIBIT 3
(Continued)

Expenses		Total	%
Personnel			
Salaries and Wages..............	$	910,676	50.9
Employee Benefits..............		136,601	7.6
Overtime		22,919	1.3
Teacher Fees..................		29,195	1.6
Total Personnel.............		1,099,391	61.4
Administrative/Program			
Accounting/Legal Fees...........		36,758	2.1
Advertising...................		30,705	1.7
Computer Service..............		16,867	0.9
Conservation		29,732	1.7
Consultant/Artist Fees...........		68,658	3.8
Cost of Goods Sold.............		40,873	2.3
Drayage.....................		11,678	0.7
Dues/Subscriptions		5,839	0.3
Equipment Repair Rental..........		7,785	0.4
Insurance		41,141	2.3
Postage		20,705	1.2
Printing......................		58,390	3.3
Receptions/Food		15,839	0.9
Security Fees..................		12,919	0.7
Supplies/Materials		71,041	4.0
Workshops/Travel/Meetings		29,463	1.6
Other.......................		11,678	0.6
Total Administrative/Program...		510,071	28.5
Maintenance/Utilities			
Maintenance		26,544	1.5
Telephone		18,490	1.0
Gas		63,088	3.5
Electric		70,873	4.0
Taxes/Water & Sewage..........		1,186	0.1
Total Maintenance/Utilities.....		180,181	10.1
Total Expenses	$	1,789,643	100.0
Surplus (Deficit)	$	(87,175)	

EXHIBIT 4
Henrik Arts Center Line Budget
(1st Estimate) July 1, 1984 to June 30, 1985

Revenues		Total	%
Earned			
Shops	$	105,000	5.7
Tuition/Class Fees		43,300	2.3
Admission/Ticket Sales		168,000	9.0
Fees/Commissions		20,000	1.1
Trips/Workshops		11,400	0.6
Endowment		188,500	10.2
Other Income		21,000	1.2
Total Earned		557,200	30.1
Grants			
City		35,000	1.9
County		108,000	5.8
State		75,600	4.1
Federal		45,800	2.5
Private		29,200	1.6
Total Grants		293,600	15.9
Contributions			
Individuals—Annual Giving		205,000	11.1
Corporations/Foundations		750,000	40.5
Memberships		45,200	2.4
Total Contributions		1,000,200	54.0
Total Revenues	$	1,851,000	100.0

EXHIBIT 4
(Continued)

Expenses	Total	%
Personnel		
Salaries and Wages.	$ 990,000	49.3
Employee Benefits.	168,300	8.4
Overtime	25,000	1.3
Teacher Fees.	32,800	1.6
Total Personnel.	1,216,100	60.6
Administrative/Program		
Accounting/Legal Fees.	40,000	1.9
Advertising	38,000	1.9
Computer Service.	18,000	0.9
Conservation	31,000	1.5
Consultant/Artist Fees.	71,200	3.5
Cost of Goods Sold.	53,300	2.7
Drayage	13,300	0.7
Dues/Subscriptions	7,300	0.4
Equipment Repair Rental.	9,000	0.5
Insurance	41,800	2.1
Postage	22,200	1.1
Printing.	69,900	3.5
Receptions/Food	16,300	0.8
Security Fees.	13,900	0.7
Supplies/Materials	78,100	3.9
Workshops/Travel/Meetings	32,600	1.6
Other	40,000	2.0
Total Administrative/Program. . .	595,900	29.7
Maintenance/Utilities		
Maintenance	29,100	1.4
Telephone	21,500	1.1
Gas	69,200	3.4
Electric	74,200	3.7
Taxes/Water & Sewage.	1,200	0.1
Total Maintenance/Utilities.	195,200	9.7
Total Expenses	$ 2,007,200	100.0
Surplus (Deficit)	$ (156,200)	

Chicago, and James Brown has recently been hired as the new director of the Henrik Arts Center. In less than a month, the first budget proposals for the following fiscal year will be reviewed by the board.

In Brown's first few weeks, he has identified several basic problems which disturb him and require his immediate attention. First, as shown in Exhibit 3, there is an operating deficit of $87,175 projected for the end of the 1984 fiscal year. Second, he lacks the financial information he needs in order to decipher the current year's deficit, let alone to assist him in the preparation of the 1985 budget. Third, the board has not given him much guidance regarding program goals upon which to build the budget. Finally, the chairman of the board in a recent phone conversation indicated that he is extremely uncomfortable with the lack of financial information and the fact that no clear vision of the organization's future is spelled out. The chairman doesn't understand what the future holds for the Henrik Arts Center and wants the budget proposal to address these issues.

The board of trustees is clearly uneasy. After a period of growth in which income continued to rise and funds were readily found to support increasing expenditures, they are concerned that resources will not be adequate in the future to maintain the exhibit programs. They are also worried about community reaction if the museum disposes of large traveling exhibitions in order to make room for a permanent collection exhibition series.

Brown has begun to develop his plans for next year, which include preparation of a budget as requested by the board for its December meeting. His first attempt at a budget is shown in Exhibit 4.

Although each item taken alone seems reasonable to him, he is disturbed by the bottom line. The projected deficit of $156,200 is a shock and would clearly be unacceptable to the board. In reviewing the proposed budget figures, Brown notes that approximately 61 percent of the expenditures are for salaries, wages, and benefits. Other expenditures are distributed among a number of items, none of which is larger than 3.9 percent of the total. What is he to do to solve this dilemma?

The budget as first prepared is certainly unacceptable. A number of key questions immediately arise:

1. Are revenue projections achievable?
2. Are additional sources of revenue possible—raising fees, exerting extra efforts on existing activities, initiating new fundraising programs, providing new services?
3. Can expenditures be reduced by cutting certain costs?
4. Can alternative approaches be used to improve efficiency and effectiveness and thereby lower costs with limited effects on services?

The challenge for management is to identify and examine all the variables that might permit the Henrik Arts Center to increase revenue and reduce expenditures. It is essential that the revenue/cost equation at least be in balance; if possible, an excess of revenues (a surplus) should be produced to provide for uncertainties in future periods. The chapters that follow describe some of the key financial management tools that can be applied in the Henrik case to arrive at the intended financial objective.

3

Strategic Planning

For arts organizations such as the Henrik Arts Center, one of the most critical management processes involves thinking carefully about the future. Governing boards, directors, and senior staff need to examine organizational purpose in light of many changing factors that may affect the future. The concerns expressed by the board of the Henrik Arts Center, coupled with an impending financial deficit of some significance, requires some careful thought by the director, James Brown. To act precipitously to balance the budget may cause more harm than good. Brown believes that he must consider various alternatives to arrive at a strategy for Henrik. He decides that he must learn more about strategic thinking and planning. Accordingly, he begins to do some research, speaking to other directors and professional consultants familiar with the subject. The following summarizes some of what he learned.

STRATEGIC PLANNING DEFINED

Strategic planning is the means used to consider future options and make decisions about organizational direction. Strategic planning provides a perspective for the review of mission, goals, objectives, and programs and the related use of available resources. Frequently, organizations slip unaware into an untenable position regarding long-held views and, in some cases, commitments. An art museum, for example, founded as a showcase for original paintings of top quality, may wish to continue its acquisition of important works as they become available. But if the funds available to the museum are now completely inadequate to support the continued purchase of such paintings in the current market, the museum must either revise its basic purpose or suffer ignominy in its decline. Such basic issues must be faced in the strategic plan. If a fundamental reduction of the arts organization's scope is necessary, a major function of the plan—perhaps over a five-year period in the above case—is to provide an orderly transition and to set forth from year to year the required program changes. At the same time, the plan should identify new sources of revenue, current outlays that are no longer necessary, and estimated costs of the new programs. Similarly, if a ballet company is undergoing significant expansion to serve new or increased audiences, the strategic plan enables the organization to grow in a controlled and orderly fashion. It provides boundaries within which to allocate resources when making budgetary decisions.

STRATEGIC PLANNING PROCESS

Strategic planning prepares trustees and administrators for dealing with the future. Although it is the most difficult task they will face, it is the most important element in the management process. Its intent is to avoid precipitous action by spelling out what should be done and to prepare in advance for changes in plans that may be necessary to cope with the foreseen and unforeseen future. When performed and implemented effectively, strategic planning serves as a guide in making decisions about the future.

Some administrators maintain that they can operate effectively without planning—even though many who have tried to do so have failed. "After all," they ask, "how can you predict the future with certainty? Why waste our time?" Furthermore, for some reason, people have difficulty coping with the abstractions of the future. It is easier to deal with the here and now: One can size up the problem and decide what to do because it is there. If the future *must* be dealt with, surely there is more certainty with the immediate future—the next hour, day, week, or month.

Clearly, however, when one makes decisions based on such a short-term perspective, there are constraints that often cannot be changed so quickly, and options that are no longer available because the opportunity to act has long since passed. In making short-range decisions, trustees and administrators—unable to act aggressively—react with whatever means remain at their disposal. Too often the only choice is between accepting a deficit and making a feeble attempt at increasing revenue by emergency fundraising and ruthless cost-cutting which may severely damage artistic programs. In the case of the Henrik Arts Center, this is certainly one option available to James Brown as he deals with his organization's deficit problem.

The planning process does not purport to predict the future. Precision is not intended. Rather, the intent is to decide what should be done, to determine how it should be accomplished, and to consider alternative actions that may be required if original plans do not work out precisely as anticipated.

The planning process involves distinct activities designed to encourage careful thinking about an arts organization's future direction. Exhibit 5 presents an overview of the planning process activities which are described as follows:

1. Assess the current state of the organization. In order to plan, trustees and administrators must understand how the organization currently operates. Based on an analysis of recent history, such questions should be raised: What artistic offerings have been provided? What audiences have been served, what were their characteristics, and how well did we serve them? What artists were used, and were we satisfied with their performances or the quality of art? What is the status of the support staff, how many volunteers were used, and were their talents used most effectively? How do our facilities support the art form, what shortcomings exist, and what improvements were made? Finally, what were the financial results of artistic activities, and has our financial condition improved or deteriorated?

These questions lead to an understanding of the use of past resources, i.e., program, audience, staff and volunteers, facilities, and finances. Such an understanding is useful

EXHIBIT 5
Model for Strategic Planning

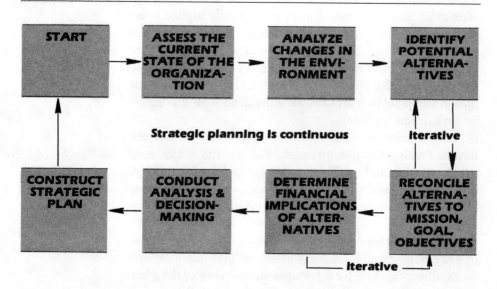

because planned changes will directly affect the way the organization uses these resources in the future.

2. Analyze changes in the environment. Arts organizations are affected by the environment and, accordingly, must consider how environmental conditions will affect their future affairs. Environmental factors include conditions in the social, economic, political, cultural, and physical milieu in which an arts organization operates, but over which it has no direct control. Examples of environmental factors are:

- the pattern of giving to the arts nationally;
- the level of categorical program support by sources available to the arts;
- the attitude of people toward the arts;
- the number of people receiving program services from arts organizations in the nation and the region.

Some of these factors may have substantial consequences for planning, but because arts organizations cannot change the environment, they must adapt. The effect of various environmental scenarios upon a preferred course of action should be tested against two or more possible sets of environmental factors.

3. Identify potential alternatives. Trustees and arts administrators are faced with making decisions regarding the future of arts organizations and specific programs to be offered. These decisions are usually made after considering potential alternatives. For instance, the Henrik Museum may consider whether it should mount a show featuring regional arts and crafts or a traveling exhibit of contemporary American paintings, while the Hudson River Ballet Company might assess the merits of a summer season versus a regional tour. These alternatives are different means of achieving a specified end.

4. Reconcile alternatives to mission, goals, and objectives. In most cases, trustees and administrators generally understand an arts organization's mission, goals, and objectives, even when they are not explicitly stated. They are the organization's reason for being, and when made explicit, they identify what the organization seeks to accomplish. Years ago, one means of resource allocation involved using a methodology referred to as Programming, Planning and Budgeting System (PPBS), in which explicit statements of mission and program goals and objectives are established before alternatives are considered. Defining mission, goals, and objectives, however, has proved difficult because such concepts are elusive. Too often, such an exercise has proved futile as people become frustrated trying to come up with "the right language." As a result, the planning process never continues beyond that point.

Another, more successful, approach has been first to decide what should change and then to identify and define available alternatives in concrete statements. Discussions of these statements leads to consideration of how the alternatives support, or conflict with, the organization's basic purpose. Out of this process evolves a clarification of organization mission, goals and objectives. Most importantly, each proposed alternative's value is reconciled to mission, goals and objectives. This may mean that potential alternatives must be modified or that one or more new alternatives be developed. This form of feedback loop establishes a necessary iterative process to assure that feasible alternatives that support the arts organization's purposes are proposed.

5. Determine financial implications of the alternatives. Obviously, a key element in deciding what should be done in the future is to consider the expected financial consequences of the alternatives. (A schematic diagram of the projection process is shown in Exhibit 6.) Development of financial projections requires consideration of the current state of institutional operations, the changes that would be required by each alternative, and the effect of the sets of environmental assumptions on the future. Where relevant, multiple projec-

EXHIBIT 6
The Projection Process

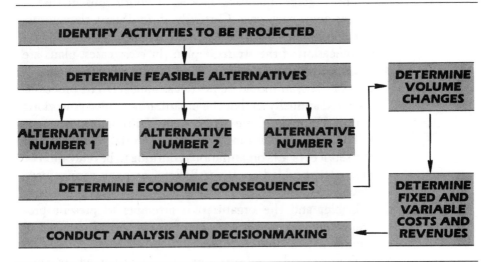

tions may be made for each alternative by varying the volume of expected audience demand. This identifies the sensitivity of cost and revenue to changes in demand. These projections help trustees and administrators to understand the breakeven point of each alternative, which is essential in determining future financial implications.

Again, the planning effort at this point attempts to determine the feasibility of proposed alternatives from a financial perspective as opposed to focusing all attention on defining the mission, goals and objectives. If an alternative is determined not to be feasible financially, the process proposes a feedback loop which re-examines the merits of the alternative.

6. Conduct analysis and decisionmaking. By considering the artistic merits of alternatives, as well as the related financial and other resource implications, trustees and arts administrators can decide which alternatives most closely satisfy the future needs of the organization. These decisions establish the parameters that guide the organization during the planning period.

The strategic planning process is continuous in that it begins anew each year. Certainly, if significant changes occur during the year, it may be advantageous to institute a modification of the strategic plan. In most cases, plans are developed for three to five years into the future. The first year of the plan should be next year's budget. The process is repeated annually so that the organization is always working within a moving, three- to five-year planning horizon.

The strategic planning process is essential to ensure that the services of arts organizations continue to be relevant. For example, the Hudson River Ballet Company cannot continue unless audiences perceive its mission and purpose as valuable, and the organization attempts to present programs that capture the interest of its public within the constraints of available resources.

Trustees and administrators must consider whom they serve and how the arts organization can best present its services in a manner that satisfies needs. The planning process focuses attention on these key issues so that the activities of arts organizations can change to meet the needs of a changing society.

ENVIRONMENTAL ANALYSIS

Environmental analysis (illustrated in Exhibit 7) is an essential part of the planning process. It is composed of two primary parts: macroenvironmental and microenvironmental analysis. Each organization must assess how the environment is likely to affect them over the next three to five years. The environmental factors discussed in the following section are illustrative but representative of the key factors that are applicable to most arts organizations. A matrix of these key environmental factors is presented in Exhibit 8.

Macroenvironmental Analysis

The macroenvironmental analysis focuses on the big picture. For an arts organization, this analysis should include consideration of relevant economic, demographic, sociocultural, political, regulatory, and technological factors.

The following questions suggest the type of macroenvironmental issues most arts organizations should address.

1. Economic
a) What is the current state of the economy and what are the forecasts for the future?
b) What is the inflation rate?

2. Demographic
a) What are the present characteristics and projected trends of national population growth?
b) What is the present and projected age distribution of the population?
c) Are there trends indicating significant regional shifts of the population?

EXHIBIT 7
Model for Environment Analysis

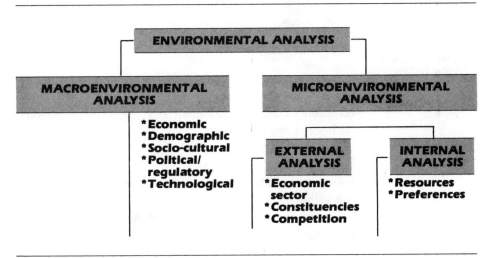

EXHIBIT 8
Examples of Key Environmental Factors
for Arts Organizations

MACRO-ENVIRONMENTAL	MICROENVIRONMENTAL	
	External	Internal
1. Economic • State of economy • Inflation rate **2. Demographic** • Population growth • Age distribution • Regional population shifts • Population preferences—arts **3. Socio-cultural** • Attitude toward arts • Career and personal trends • Value reorientation • Consumer demands **4. Political/Regulatory** • Government regulations • Accreditation requirements • Political climate for the arts • Legislative proposals **5. Technological** • New technology	**1. Economic Sector** • Price and cost trends for arts • Economics of scale • Capacity • Price competition • Price elasticity of demand **2. Constituencies** • Major audiences • Segmentation • New targets • Size and growth trend • Local perceptions • Factors influencing decisions **3. Competition** • Competitive organizations • Competitor strengths and weaknesses • Competitor future strategies • New competition • Indirect competition	**1. Resources** • Quality and flexibility • Staff turnover • Senior staff capability • Middle management capability • Fundraising and community relations • Sources of revenue • Condition/capacity—physical plant • Role of board **2. Preferences** • Board • Staff • Artists • Audience

d) What are the characteristics of the population with respect to cultural attainment (e.g., percent of persons with some arts exposure)?

3. Socio-Cultural

a) What are society's current and emerging attitudes about the values and purposes of the arts?

b) What are the trends in career expectations and personal life-styles?

c) Is there evidence of significant value reorientation in the society?

d) What are the consumer demands on the arts?

4. Political/Regulatory

a) What expected changes in governmental regulation will affect organizational compliance practices?

b) What are the concerns of national/regional accrediting bodies?

c) What is the political climate regarding the place of the arts in American society?

d) Are there significant legislative proposals that would have an impact on the arts?

5. Technological

Are there new technological developments or new applications of present technology that suggest alternative means of conducting the arts program?

With respect to the future, a macroenvironmental analysis with a three- to five-year time horizon is recommended. Assumptions made for many of the environmental factors are inevitably subject to error, generally in proportion to their time horizons; beyond five years, assumptions are often of dubious validity.

After the macroenvironmental analysis has been completed, its implications should be determined. Specifically, this involves identifying the opportunities and threats confronting the organization as a result of macroenvironmental factors. For example, an expected increase in the number of Americans with a diversity of interest in the arts may afford the organization an opportunity to establish new programs. However, if limited resources are available, new programs may pose a threat to existing programs, and difficult choices will have to be made.

Microenvironmental Analysis

The microenvironmental analysis is subdivided into two

separate evaluations: external and internal. The first includes analyses of the economic sector (i.e., the arts) within which the institution functions, the institution's current or potential constituencies, and competition. The internal analysis assesses the institution's resources (programmatic, artistic, audience, physical, and financial) and the preferences of various individuals or groups within it.

Beginning with the external analysis, the following questions are helpful in assessing the economic sector, constituencies, and competition:

1. External analysis
a) Economic sector
- What are the price and cost trends in the arts?
- Are there significant economies of scale (i.e., does organizational size relate significantly to operating efficiency)?
- Is there presently or will there in the near future be excess capacity to meet the demand for cultural services?
- What is the price range of competing arts programs?
- What is the price elasticity of demand (i.e., to what extent is demand affected by changes in price)?

b) Constituencies
- What are the organization's major audience constituencies (e.g., local, regional, statewide)?
- What is the most useful segmentation of each of the major constituencies? For example, the local community might be grouped according to geographical origin, age, art interest, full-time/part-time employment, church affiliation, etc.
- What potential new target constituencies or segments can be identified?
- What is the size and growth trend of each major constituency and segment?
- How do artists, members of the community, financial supporters, etc., perceive the arts organization?
- How do the audience and financial supporters make

their decisions (i.e., what factors influence attendance and financial support decision)?

c) **Competition**
- What are the major competitive organizations?
- What are the strengths and weaknesses of these institutions (e.g., reputation, price, staff, range of programs, finances, administration, location and location appeal)?
- What are the likely present and future strategies of these organizations?
- Are there sources of potential new competition?
- What are the sources of indirect competition for each major constituency (e.g., amount of leisure time available for adults)?

2. Internal analysis

a) **Resources**
- What is the quality and flexibility of the staff (e.g., ability to adapt to or create new programs)?
- What is the predicted rate of staff turnover?
- How capable is the senior staff?
- What are the strengths and weaknesses of middle management?
- How effective are the organization's external operations, in fundraising and community relations?
- What is the financial status of the organization, including relationships with lending institutions?
- What are the sources of revenue for the arts organization?
- What is the condition and capacity of the organization's physical plant?
- Does the board of trustees play an effective role?

b) **Preferences**
The preference analysis lets various members of the organization (board, staff, artists, and audience) contribute to the planning process by revealing their hopes and desires. Since the success of an arts organization depends on the personal commitment of the members of

its community, it is important to pay attention to their subjective wishes, as well as to the objective constraints and opportunities in the environment. Coordinating preferences through existing vehicles, such as committees, may be the best approach.

An environmental analysis, also referred to as an "environmental scan," is an essential tool for enabling administrators and trustees to understand the relevance of existing and proposed programs on the organization's constituency. By providing an understanding of the interests of the various constituencies served, such a scan will often significantly influence decisions about which programs to emphasize and how resources should be used.

THE PLANNING PROCESS ILLUSTRATED: THE HENRIK ARTS CENTER

Now that he understands the strategic planning process, James Brown decides that he should begin to initiate strategic planning at the Henrik Arts Center. He realizes that he must give some creative thought to the future of the arts center. Many decisions were made by his entrepreneurial predecessor—some good and some bad. However, some things have changed; the Henrik Arts Center has emerged with new sources of money, but with an unclear vision of its role and the linkage of its parts into a cohesive whole. Accordingly, Brown proposes to establish a formal planning process. Time being of the essence, he concludes that for the first attempt at strategic planning he cannot afford such a luxury and therefore must proceed with planning and budgeting simultaneously.

Brown concludes that a successful planning process requires implementation or action if it is to accomplish desirable change. Accordingly, the initial involvement of those who will be instrumental in the implementation pro-

cess—key staff members, board members, and active volunteers—is important. With this in mind, he forms a planning
team composed of his administrative cabinet to analyze
present conditions and competition and to formulate future
directions for the arts center. He also establishes an advisory
committee to provide advice and counsel to the planning
team regarding proposed strategies and directions. This committee is composed of selected members of the board and a
cross-section of volunteers from the community familiar
with the arts center and its activities. The committee will be
chaired by the chairman of the board's budget and finance
committee.

Brown calls the first meeting of the planning committee.
At the meeting, he explains the charge of the committee
and indicates his desire to have a completed draft plan for
presentation to the board's budget and finance committee in
six months. Further, it is his wish that the planning process
influence this year's budget as it is prepared. Brown indicates
that the committee will initially meet bi-weekly, with the
schedule changing as materials are prepared for discussion
and decisionmaking. He appoints his administrative assistant as planning officer, in whom he assigns the responsibility for documenting discussion and decisions, and for preparing the strategic plan under the direction of the committee.

As a first effort, he proposes that two areas of emphasis be
considered by the committee. First, he wishes to assess the
macro and micro environment to prepare assumptions about
the next five-year period. He proceeds to lead the discussion
assessing each of the following areas:
- economic
- demographic
- socio-cultural
- political/regulatory
- technological

The discussion is far ranging but seems to highlight
important changes that the Henrik Arts Center must
recognize as it prepares for the future. Similar preliminary

discussion continues on the micro-environment from an external perspective. The discussion focuses on:

- economic sector
- constituencies
- competition

The planning officer participates actively in the discussion and records the key points made by the members of the team. Brown requests that the planning officer distribute the key points to the members so they may give further thought to the environment. In addition, the planning officer is assigned to visit the library and to contact the state arts agency and other key associations in the arts in order to collect and assimilate key information about the environment for the next meeting. This information is to be distributed two days beforehand so that all team members can study the materials and prepare for the next discussion.

The second major task involves further analysis by the planning officer regarding the arts center's resources and preferences. Brown requests that the head of the fundraising department assist in performing the preference analysis. This would involve using a questionnaire which would be shared with staff, board, and a cross-section of the community. He requests that the results be available for discussion in six weeks. Brown also asks the planning officer, with the business manager, to prepare an analysis of the arts center's resources which details strengths and weaknesses. This will require interviews with members of the planning committee and others as necessary. The results of the resource assessment should be ready for discussion in one month.

Once these tasks are completed, a weekend planning retreat will be conducted. The purposes of this retreat will be to identify alternative actions that should be considered and to define the appropriate strategy—to include a clear statement of mission, goals, and objectives for the Henrik Arts Center over the next five years. When completed, a written draft of the plan—including assessments of the environment and of the arts center's strengths and weaknesses, the proposed five-year strategy including mission, goals, and objectives, and an action plan—will be prepared for discussion and approval by the board and for possible presentation to the community.

While the five-year strategic plan is being prepared, the budget for next year will also be prepared. Out of the plan will come some determination of areas for emphasis or de-emphasis, which in the first year should be considered by Brown in leading the budget preparation effort and in the evaluation of budget requests.

The next chapter describes the budget preparation process with its initial results. James Brown is most concerned with understanding how each division director proposes to assign resources. He expects for this first year to use these budget submissions as the primary basis for discussions and modification. However, in every case, he also plans to consider the strategic directions of the new plan as he evaluates each budget request.

4

Budgeting

THE BUDGETING PROCESS is a key step in the overall management process in that it is used to make decisions about how resources will be allocated to accomplish organizational mission, goals, and objectives. At the Henrik Arts Center, James Brown is dissatisfied with the historical approach to budgeting. He believes that insufficient information is developed during the budget process to permit effective evaluation and decisionmaking. He realizes that the arts center has grown significantly in size with little change in its budgeting practices. He again decides to do some research to understand what approach he should apply at the Henrik Arts Center.

Budget preparation follows planning and defines in detail how available resources will be used to accomplish the strategic plan. A well-designed budget serves as a reference tool when:

1. Making resource allocation decisions (proceeding with implementation and operating on a day-to-day basis)
2. Monitoring progress (exercising control)
3. Examining afterwards what was accomplished (evaluating performance)

Budgets are usually prepared for one year. Many boards and administrators, however, now want to see the long-term effect of decisions and are insisting that a plan be prepared first which puts the short-term view (the budget) into the context of the planned, long-term direction.

WHY DO WE BUDGET?

Budgeting in arts organizations may be characterized as a careful balancing act of trying to maximize revenues and minimize expenses to conduct programs which meet the needs of the organization's constituency. This balancing act is highlighted by the two illustrations: "Budget Iceberg" and the "Camel's Nose under the Tent."

In the "Budget Iceberg," existing programs are assumed to be part of the fundamental base of the organization. Often, they are unexamined and accepted as part of the very fiber of the organization. In contrast, proposed new programs (often modest in comparison to existing programs) are subject to close scrutiny. They are examined in excruciating detail and negotiated endlessly by staff, volunteers, and the board.

The "Camel's Nose Under the Tent" highlights the fact that an arts organization often has limited resources to fund existing programs. New programs—represented by the camel —are often trying to find room (or support) within the confines of the limitations imposed by the tent (available total resources). So the dilemma: Do you make room for new programs under the tent by throwing out existing programs, or do you strive for a bigger tent? For example, the idea of the

Hudson River Ballet Company expanding its repertory may be exciting and innovative in design. Financial constraints, however, require that new funding be received or that certain existing activities be removed so that resources may be shifted to accommodate the new repertory.

The budgeting process is an approach to resolving these questions. In a logical way, it seeks to balance programmatic needs against resource constraints. It provides a vehicle for making explicit choices—some of which may not be easy. As such, it is a means of formally documenting how resources will be used. It identifies specific actions that will be taken to increase revenues necessary to satisfy increasing demands for resources. When applied properly, the budgeting process is logically organized to arrive at careful conclusions on how to use available resources.

Budgeting is also—by nature—political. It is a representative process of people contending for scarce resources. As such, the behavior of people can become irrational, but those involved with the budgeting process must discourage irrational behavior; it is detrimental to the future of the organization.

WHAT'S WRONG WITH MOST BUDGET PROCESSES?

Emphasis on New Programs. In many cases it is assumed that old programs should continue. As a result, all attention is directed at proposed new programs.

This unbalanced emphasis serves to institutionalize existing programs, which is unwise considering the changing interests and needs of the organization's audience. All program activities should be assessed equally in the budget process to assure that knowledgeable decisions are made regarding proposed resource allocations.

Incremental/Decremental Budgeting Policy. In many arts organizations—especially nonprofit ones—the budget process begins with an estimate of revenues. The director or the business officer estimates that the total funds available next year will be, say, approximately 10 percent under the current level. Then all attention is focused on how to cut 10 percent from expenses. A related phenomenon is the conclusion that this 10 percent reduction should be equitably shared by all budget units in the organization. (In a good year, a 10 per-cent increase necessitates a similar, but less painful process.) Thus, each unit should reduce its budget by 10 percent. This process is called incremental or decremental budgeting because attention is focused on the increment or decrement —the 10 percent—rather than on the total.

The basic underlying assumptions of incremental/decre-mental budgeting are that nothing fundamental should be changed; that current funding levels for the various activ-ities are equitable and necessary; and therefore, that the budgeting process is limited to allocating the anticipated increment or decrement.

This approach to budgeting has a fatal flaw. It assumes that all budget entities should be treated equally. This should definitely not be the case. To presume that the 10 percent should be shared by all may foster equal mediocrity.

Often Prepared Late. Budgets are often prepared just before or even after the fiscal year begins. This precludes mean-ingful resource allocations since most decisions are made months before. To use the budget merely to record actions already taken is to obtain only a portion of the benefits that may be derived from the budgeting process.

Budgets should be prepared and approved by the board long before the year begins. For example, for a museum whose fiscal year begins July 1, it may be advisable to have a completed budget by the preceding January or even earlier. In this way, key decisions, such as hiring staff or committing to a show next spring, can be made within the context of the approved budget. For organizations that make major com-mitments even earlier, it may be necessary to prepare budgets as much as nine, twelve, or even eighteen months before the year begins. It is important to keep in mind that budgets are not "carved in stone." Rather, they are flexible and need to be adjusted in consideration of changing circumstances.

Lack of Participation. Frequently, budgets are prepared by one member of the professional staff. This may be the business officer, the director, or some individual designated by the director. Too often, limited discussion occurs regarding programmatic needs, the views of key staff, existing constraints, and the need for priorities. As a result, allocation decisions (or non decisions) are made without full information.

The budget should be prepared with the participation of key individuals responsible for the activities concerned. Participation is necessary to assure that the proposed budget is an accurate reflection of plans for the future. Perhaps equally important is the fact that participation encourages commitment to accomplishing the objectives that are supportive of organizational mission and goals.

Non-Comprehensive. A major difficulty with many budgets is that they narrowly focus on current unrestricted funds to the exclusion of other sources of money. This form of "cookie jar budgeting" suggests that different monies (i.e., current unrestricted funds, individual restricted funds, and capital funds) are unrelated and therefore are budgeted separately. Such an approach fails to consider the interaction of people, finances, and facilities in providing programs to audiences. For example, the Hudson River Ballet Company may prepare a budget for its regular annual season. A special program to bring dance to local schools will be funded by a foundation grant. A grant from a corporation may also be received to initiate a summer program in the park. These separate sources of funding frequently cause separate budgets to be prepared for each program. As a result, a cohesive approach to using resources is not considered and an unconnected set of activities emerges which negatively affects artistic quality and economy.

Budgets should consider the use of all sources of funds in carrying out programs. Thus, the operating budget containing current unrestricted and restricted funds should include all activities regardless of funding source. Further, the operating budget should be prepared in concert with the capital budget.

Insufficient Focus on Policy. Budgets, when finally approved, reflect the policies of an arts organization. Frequently, however, budgeting decisions are made without regard to their policy implications. This often happens in larger organizations where separate departments submit budget requests. Each budget request typically contains policy decisions. Occasionally, these proposed policy decisions are not complementary.

The budgeting process should provide a means of:
1) establishing policy guidance before budgets are prepared;
2) assessing budget policy matters across the organization; and
3) permitting policy differences to be resolved in light of organizational goals and objectives.

Key Variables Not Understood. There are two types of variables that influence future cost and revenue behavior. The first, called environmental factors (defined in the preceding chapter), are conditions in the social, economic, political, cultural, and physical milieu in which an arts organization operates, but over which it has no direct control. The second, called decision factors, are those specific attributes of goals, objectives, and programs, organizational structure, and operating policies which can be directly affected by administrative decisions. Examples are:
• changes in programs
• changes in number of staff and artists

- changes in compensation rates
- changes in the number of performances or hours open to the public

When preparing budgets, arts organizations often fail to consider the impact of these factors on the future. Yet it is the combination of these factors, and changes thereto, that can result in substantially different programmatic and budgetary outcomes for the organizations. Decision factors in particular are a powerful tool in determining future outcomes. Decision factors are the dials on the television screen referred to earlier. Each dial can be adjusted to change the picture and then bring it into focus. In the budgeting process, these dials must be adjusted to determine future direction most effectively.

Long-Range Plan Missing. Frequently, budgets are prepared without the guiding principles and parameters of a long-range strategic plan. Such a plan is necessary to serve as the context within which short-range decisions contained in the budget are made.

Responsibilities Are Unclear. There are many activities, programs, and related revenues and expenses in a budget. Too often, responsibilities for these activities are not clearly assigned when the budget is established. As a result, it is difficult to use the budget as an effective monitor of progress in achieving goals and objectives.

The budget document, when completed, should serve as a control device to assess accomplishments in light of what was planned. Responsibilities for all elements of the budget should be assigned to selected individuals.

Lack of Communication. Budgets are prepared without sufficient communication among departments regarding services to be provided. For example, plant operations and maintenance, security, computing, and other departments need to know what levels of support will be required. Frequently, there is insufficient discussion regarding expected needs and the timing of such requests.

The budget process should provide time for discussion of the expected demand for services. If it is the practice to charge for services rendered, the budgets of the provider and recipient should reflect the interdepartmental credit and charge for the service. An illustration of such services might be computing. The cost of computing might be budgeted by user departments such as the business office and fundraising. Similarly, the computing department should budget for reimbursement of cost based on expected use. This device, often referred to as a "transfer pricing" mechanism, will facilitate control over the use of computing by fixing responsibility on both the user and provider of internal services. Typically, this form of internal budgeting and charging is used by larger organizations.

Lack of Direction. Budgeting is a complex procedure that becomes more complex as the size of the organization increases. Larger organizations require standardization in terms of budget forms and procedures to permit consistency in budget preparation, review, and approval.

For some arts organizations, budgetary practices and procedures are not clearly defined, and budget instructions and forms are not readily available. It is essential that budgetary practices and materials are written and understood by all who have responsibility for budget items.

No Review Once Budget Completed. Once budgets are submitted, they should be reviewed by the director, the business officer, and others as appropriate. Frequently, adjustments are made to budget requests. Departments must be informed of the results of the budgetary review.

To attain maximum value from the budget process, it is useful to meet subsequently with those submitting budgetary requests to explain modifications. This will assist in communicating more clearly the organization's intent in achieving its goals and objectives.

No Periodic Review. In some arts organizations, the budget is "put to rest" once it is completed and approved by the board. During the year, the director, the business officer, and the board do not review how well they are doing vis-a-vis the budgeted plan.

The budget should be a tool for guiding decisions throughout the year as the arts organization proceeds to accomplish its plans. Further, the budget should serve as a device to determine status at points along the way—usually monthly. Such status reviews give indications of variances which require attention to assure that objectives are accomplished as intended or modified as required.

Line Budgets Are Prepared. Frequently, budgets are submitted indicating projected amounts to be spent on salaries, supplies, equipment, travel and the like. This is referred to as a line-item budget. The problem with such a budget is that it is not conducive to assessing the purposes for which these line items are being spent. As a result, effective dialogue regarding the decision factors implicit in each line item cannot occur.

Arts organizations need to know how much they plan to spend on people, equipment, travel, etc. They also need to prepare the budget in program form. Programs may be characterized as primary—those which provide services to clientele—or support—those which exist to help carry out primary programs.

ORGANIZATION FOR BUDGETING

Who should participate in the budgeting process and what should be their roles? Within an organization's hierarchy, budgets should be prepared from the bottom up, based on budget guidelines devised by the business officer. The director should prepare a letter to the head of each budgeted area which transmits the guidelines as well as communicates key budget parameters. This letter should set the tone for the budgeting process. A meeting with senior staff might be held by the director and business officer to discuss the budget letter and guidelines, the timetable, and the process to be followed. Senior staff, accompanied by the business officer, should meet with staff professionals and department heads to explain budget practices and answer questions as required. Throughout the budgeting process, the business officer should provide assistance as requested.

Once budgets are completed, they should first be submitted for the review and approval of the senior staff responsible. Subsequently, they should be presented to the director, who might appoint a budget review committee—composed of senior staff, board members, and volunteers—for review, modification, and approval. The director retains ultimate responsibility for completing the budget. At that point, the director is responsible for submitting the budget to the board or a designated committee, such as the budget and finance committee. The director may request the assistance of the business officer in this regard.

Readers should note that the structure of this process must be adjusted to meet the particular needs of each arts organization. Organizational size, complexity, management style, history, governance practices, and other factors should influence the way the budget structure is developed.

THE BUDGETING PROCESS ILLUSTRATED: THE HENRIK ARTS CENTER

The budgeting process is an effective tool for developing solutions to financial dilemmas. This capability can be more fully understood by again referring to the case study of the Henrik Arts Center, presented in Chapter 2. The new direc-

tor, James Brown, is faced with a first estimate budget show-
ing a potential deficit of $156,200 (see Exhibit 4 on pages
16–17). Obviously, some action must be taken to substantially reduce and preferably eliminate this budgeted deficit.
Where should he begin?

In looking at the first estimated budget, Brown finds it
difficult to relate the line item budget to the activities actually
being carried out by the Henrik Arts Center. He recognizes
that this budget is an aggregate and that the arts center is
composed of major divisions, namely:

- Museum, including the Henrik Crafts Council
- Education, and
- The Hudson River Ballet Company

Further, he realizes that each division of the arts center
carries on programs that are important activities in and of
themselves.

To begin to analyze his budget problem, he examines the
underlying budget of each division. He then selects the
museum division first for detailed analysis because it is the
largest part of the overall budget. He believes that if some
improvement in the budget problem is possible, such
improvement will likely come from this area. He looks at the
museum division budget (see Exhibit 9) which totals
$1,002,900 out of $2,007,200 in expenses. Each line item by
itself does not tell him much. He concludes that he must
examine the proposed museum division budget expenses by
program. After discussion with the museum director he identifies the following primary museum programs:

- Curatorial
- Conservation
- Exhibitions
- Crafts Council

In addition, certain support programs exist to carry out the
primary programs. These support programs are:

- Fundraising
- Division administration
- Publicity and public relations

EXHIBIT 9
Henrik Arts Center Museum Division
Expense Budget (1st Estimate)
July 1, 1984 to June 30, 1985

Personnel

	Salaries and Wages	$ 551,600
	Employee Benefits	93,700
	Overtime	15,000
	Teacher Fees	10,000
		670,300

Other

	Advertising	14,000
	Computer Service	8,000
	Conservation	21,800
	Consultant/Artist Fees	52,200
	Drayage	13,000
	Dues/Subscriptions	2,300
	Equipment Rental	200
	Insurance	84,300
	Postage	5,100
	Printing	42,500
	Receptions/Food	11,500
	Security Fees	10,000
	Supplies/Materials	38,100
	Workshops	13,100
	Travel/Meetings	9,000
	Telephone	1,700
	Other	5,800
Total Expenses		$ 1,002,900

Brown decides that he must be able to determine the cost of each of these programs. With the museum director, he proceeds to obtain the necessary information to determine the budget for each program. They are assisted by the business officer of the arts center who is responsible for requesting, collecting, and summarizing budget submissions received from each division.

Time Budget

Initially, they proceed to analyze how each employee of the museum spends his time. They ask each individual to estimate how he expects to spend his time in relation to the seven programs just noted. This is a best estimate based upon prior experience and upon objectives that reflects the emphasis planned for next year. The results of this analysis are shown in the TIME BUDGET presented in Exhibit 10.

Personnel Cost by Program

Once the time budget is completed, the personnel cost associated with each primary and support program can be determined. This is accomplished by calculating the proportionate distribution of hours assigned to each program and applying the resulting percentage to the applicable salary and wages of the personnel noted on the time budget. Benefits are distributed proportionately in relation to total salaries and wages by program. Overtime pertains to exhibitions while teachers fees relates to the activities of the Crafts Council. The result of this calculation appears as Exhibit 11, PERSONNEL COST BY PROGRAM.

Program Expenditure Budget

Brown now proceeds to prepare the PROGRAM EXPENDITURE BUDGET, shown as Exhibit 12. The first line of this budget is obtained from the last line of Exhibit 11. The proportionate distribution of salary and wage expense is calculated at this point and is then used to allocate certain expense items that pertain to all museum programs.

In analyzing each expenditure line, certain costs are determined to be directly attributable to a single program, such as advertising to the exhibitions program. Other expenditures relate to two or more programs and can be discretely identified as direct costs of each of those programs. For example, computer service is used to support fundraising and division administration. Other expenditures cannot be attributed directly to one or more primary or support programs. In such cases, an equitable allocation is made, based upon the expected benefit that will be received by each program. For example, the cost of supplies and materials cannot easily be

EXHIBIT 10
Henrik Arts Center Museum Division
Time Budget (First Estimate)
July 1, 1984–June 30, 1985

| | PRIMARY PROGRAMS | | | | SUPPORT PROGRAMS | | | |
Position	Curatorial	Conservation	Exhibitions	Crafts Council	Publicity & Pub. Rel.	Fund-raising	Division Admin.	Total Days
Full Time Staff								
Director	10 (4%)	10 (4%)	20 (9%)	10 (4%)	20 (9%)	55 (23%)	110 (47%)	235
Asst. Director	20 (9%)	20 (9%)	40 (17%)	40 (17%)	5 (2%)	30 (12%)	80 (34%)	235
Curator—Weaving	90 (37%)	20 (9%)	65 (28%)	60 (26%)				235
Curator—Pottery	80 (34%)	30 (12%)	85 (37%)	40 (17%)				235
Curator—Mtl./Furn.	90 (38%)	45 (19%)	80 (34%)	20 (9%)				235
Curator—Macrame	100 (43%)	50 (21%)	85 (36%)					235
Asst.Curators—4	200 (21%)	300 (32%)	340 (36%)	100 (11%)				940
Senior Guard	100 (43%)		135 (57%)					235
Guards—3	350 (50%)		355 (50%)					705
Secretaries—3	235 (33%)			80 (11%)	200 (29%)	40 (6%)	150 (21%)	705
Handymen—3		300 (43%)	405 (57%)					705
Publicity Aide					235 (100%)			235

								Total Hrs.
Part-Time Staff								
Guards			2500 (100%)					2500
Porters	900 (29%)		2200 (71%)					3100

EXHIBIT 11
Henrik Arts Center Museum Division
Personnel Cost by Program
July 1, 1984–June 30, 1985

Position	PRIMARY PROGRAMS				SUPPORT PROGRAMS			Total
	Curatorial	Conservation	Exhibitions	Crafts Council	Publicity & Pub. Rel.	Fund-raising	Division Admin.	
Full Time Staff								
Director	$ 2,120	2,120	4,770	2,120	4,770	12,190	24,910	53,000
Asst. Director	3,600	3,600	6,800	6,800	800	4,800	13,600	40,000
Curator—Weaving	15,540	3,780	11,760	10,920				42,000
Curator—Pottery	14,960	5,280	16,280	7,480				44,000
Curator—Mtl./Furn.	14,440	7,220	12,920	3,420				38,000
Curator—Macrame	15,050	7,350	12,600					35,000
Asst. Curators—4	18,480	28,160	31,680	9,680				88,000
Senior Guard	9,460		12,540					22,000
Guards—3	25,500		25,500					51,000
Secretaries—3	14,850			4,950	13,050	2,700	9,450	45,000
Handymen—3		19,780	26,220					46,000
Publicity Aide					19,000			19,000
Part-Time Staff								
Guards			16,000					16,000
Porters		3,650	8,950					12,600
	134,000	80,940	186,020	45,370	37,620	19,690	47,960	551,600
	(24%)	(15%)	(34%)	(8%)	(7%)	(3%)	(9%)	(100%)
Employee Benefits	22,488	14,055	31,858	7,496	6,559	2,811	8,433	93,700
Overtime			15,000					15,000
Teacher Fees				10,000				10,000
TOTAL	$ 156,488	94,995	232,878	62,866	44,179	22,501	56,393	670,300

EXHIBIT 12
Henrik Arts Center Museum Division
Program Expenditure Budget (First Estimate)
July 1, 1984–June 30, 1985

Expenditure Item	PRIMARY PROGRAMS				SUPPORT PROGRAMS			Total
	Curatorial	Conservation	Exhibitions	Crafts Council	Publicity & Pub. Rel.	Fund-raising	Division Admin.	
Personnel	$ 156,488	94,995	232,878	62,866	44,179	22,501	56,393	670,300
Advertising			14,000					14,000
Computer Service						5,000	3,000	8,000
Conservation		21,800						21,800
Consult./Artist Fees	21,000	15,000	11,200	5,000				52,200
Drayage			13,000					13,000
Dues/Subscriptions	1,400						900	2,300
Equipment Rental			200					200
Insurance			79,000				5,300	84,300
Postage			3,400		400	1,000	300	5,100
Printing			26,500		11,000	5,000		42,500
Receptions/Food						11,500		11,500
Security Fees			10,000					10,000
Supplies/Materials	8,763	5,334	13,335	3,429	2,667	1,143	3,429	38,100
Workshops				13,100				13,100
Travel/Meetings	3,000		4,000				2,000	9,000
Telephone	391	238	595	153	119	51	153	1,700
Other	1,334	812	2,030	522	406	174	522	5,800
TOTAL	$ 192,376	138,179	410,138	85,070	58,771	46,369	71,997	1,002,900

EXHIBIT 13
Henrik Arts Center Museum Division
Revenue Budget (First Estimate)
July 1, 1984–June 30, 1985

Source	Curatorial	Conser-vation	Exhibi-tions	Crafts Council	General Purposes*	Total
Earned						
Tuition/Class Fees				43,300		43,300
Admission/Ticket Sales			99,000			99,000
Fees/Commissions			20,000			20,000
Trips/Workshops			500	10,900		11,400
Endowment	$ 58,500					58,500
Other Income	1,500	3,000	2,500			7,000
Grants						
City	30,000		5,000			35,000
County	31,600					31,600
State	800		14,800			15,600
Federal			10,800			10,800
Contributions						
Individuals—Annual Giving	20,000			35,000	67,500	122,500
Corporations/Foundations			200,000		242,500	442,500
TOTAL	$ 142,400	3,000	352,600	89,200	310,000	897,200

*Available to all purposes of Henrik Arts Center. Amount shown is allocated to Museum Division for analytic purposes.

identified directly with the benefitting programs. In this case, the proportional distribution of personnel costs is used on the assumption that each program benefits from this cost in relation to the people effort associated with each program. It is important to note that allocations are imprecise and arbitrary approximations of cost benefit. Other examples of cost allocation bases are square feet of space occupied and number of telephones assigned to each program. Whatever allocation base is used, it should bear some rational relationship to the benefits received by programs.

Revenue Budget

Once the program cost is determined, Brown decides to determine the revenue that is attributable to each program. He is interested in comparing direct museum division revenue to museum expenditures.

Exhibit 13 presents the museum division revenue budget. The REVENUE BUDGET is determined by attributing self-generated revenues earned by a program or received to support a program. All indirect revenue, i.e., revenue applicable to all museum programs is recorded in the general purposes column.

Budget Analysis

Brown compares the program revenue budget with the program expense budget. The results are shown on the following page.

It appears that two-thirds of the Henrik Arts Center's proposed first budget deficit is derived from the museum division. Although Brown has not reduced the deficit, he now has the ability to examine each program of the museum division.

Brown has similar budget details, including the time budget, program expense budget, and revenue budget, prepared for each division. He plans to meet with each division head to discuss ways to reduce expenditures and/or increase revenues to achieve equilibrium.

	Expend.	Revenues	Net
Curatorial.	$ 192,376	142,400	(49,976)
Conservation	138,179	3,000	(135,179)
Exhibitions	410,138	352,600	(57,538)
Crafts Council.	85,070	89,200	4,130
TOTAL PRIMARY PROGRAMS	825,763	587,200	(238,563)
Publicity and Public Relations.	58,771	—	(58,771)
Fundraising	46,369	—	(46,369)
Division Administration	71,997	—	(71,997)
General Purposes Revenue.	—	310,000	310,000
TOTAL SUPPORT PROGRAMS	177,137	310,000	132,863
TOTAL ALL PROGRAMS	$ 1,002,900	897,200	(105,700)

Brown now has before him just about all the information he needs to face intelligently the hard decisions implicit in the revised budget he must put together. His task is now to figure out a way to maintain the forward motion of the Henrik Arts Center and still present a realistic balanced budget for 1984–85.

5

Organization

AN ARTS ORGANIZATION DEFINES its purpose through the development of a mission statement. The planning and budgeting process, described in the previous chapters, specifies the resources—artistically and financially—necessary to achieve the goals and objectives comprised in the mission statement. Organization is the process of directing people to carry out assigned activities in pursuit of overall goals and objectives. These activities, specified in the plan of action, cannot be accomplished without people resources. Therefore, board, staff, and volunteers are a vital linkage which must be structured effectively and efficiently if an arts organization is to be successful.

Such structuring is an essential part of a well-conceived financial management process. The need for accountability and separation of duties to establish effective internal controls are critical elements of sound financial management. Thus, the organization of people to perform their responsibilities also must carefully consider key financial management practices in concert with appropriate organizational principles.

The observations in this chapter relate to the structure of an arts organization and the framework that structure provides for smooth, efficient, and productive operation. These observations are based upon principles which reflect the standards that an arts organization must meet to achieve its goals and objectives. Generic in nature, these criteria were derived from both accepted organizational theory and from experience.

Initially, the chapter describes key principles that should be considered when organizing or reorganizing. Possible alternative organization structures are then presented. The use of the job description as an important device for defining roles and responsibility is also discussed. Finally, a description of the typical structure of an organization's financial function is provided to serve as a guide in establishing effective financial management responsibilities for arts organizations.

KEY ORGANIZATION PRINCIPLES

Is it necessary that an organization have a formal structure? What is the best structure? Who should report to whom? These questions are often difficult to answer, yet they must be clearly resolved. The moment more than one person is involved in a joint activity, dance, theatre, museum exhibitions, etc., there is a need to organize—to agree to share responsibilities. Decisions about who will do what are based on many factors, including personal strengths, weaknesses, and interests, but there are a number of fundamental organization principles that should be understood before establishing a new organization or modifying the structure of an existing one. These principles, discussed below, serve as a reference when deciding on the best structure for an organization and on who should report to whom.

Separation of Responsibilities

Implicit in this principle is the assumption that the responsibilities of board and staff are separate and distinct. Theoretically, the distinction might be made along very broad lines: The business of the board of trustees is policy; the business of the director and staff is operations. In practice, however, such absolute distinctions are misleading for a number of reasons.

First, there is uncertainty about what constitutes "policy." In general terms, policy involves deciding on overall directions and issues affecting the affairs of an organization. One example would be the decision by the board of a dance company to establish an affiliation with another dance company in order to conduct programs at a single shared site. In contrast, operations is the implementation of policy—for example, specific decisions about scheduling the use of facilities for practice or performance.

Second, there are different levels of policy. For example, the board in the case just noted might focus attention on broad strategic policy, such as the affiliation agreement. In another organization, the board might be concerned with establishing policy at lower levels, such as setting a fixed dollar level of proposed expenditures (e.g., $5,000) which must be approved by the treasurer of the board before payment is authorized. In some organizations, such lower level policies are left to the discretion of management. The size and complexity of the organization (and complexity is not simply a function of size)—as well as whether it is public or private, its history, and the style of the individuals involved —largely determine the levels of policy at which the trustees, director, and subordinates properly perform.

Beyond this, however, the trustees must determine both the level of policy at which they will operate and the level at which the director will be allowed to operate. The director must make a similar determination between his own policy role and that which will be delegated to subordinates.

Finally, there are certain operations properly performed by the board—fundraising, for example, which is a particular activity *undertaken* by the board in pursuit of policy *set* by the board. In such a case, trustees both set and implement policy. Another example might be the selection of the director. The process of selection—including discussions related to organizational goals, the role of the director, his or her relationship to the board, and other matters—is an articulation of established or proposed policy. Thus, the ultimate decision regarding the selection of the director is both an assertion of board policy and the implementation of that policy.

Such activities demonstrate that the respective roles of the board and the director are not defined simply by the distinction between policy and implementation. A similar statement can be made regarding the role of the director vis-a-vis subordinates.

It appears, then, that two of the most universally accepted functions of trustees—soliciting funds and selecting the director—are acts of implementation in pursuit of policy. In both cases, the trustees must also set the policies to be pursued. It must be concluded, then, that the distribution of responsibilities among the trustees, the director, and the staff do not fall neatly into the categories of policymaking and implementation. Rather, the following, more complex distinctions are proposed:

1. In arts organizations, policymaking is a shared responsibility of trustees, director, and staff. The trustees have final responsibility for policy governing the use of resources—people, facilities, equipment, finances, programs, and audiences. Beyond this, there are levels of policy appropriate to each aspect of the organization's affairs, and the board must set the level of policy at which it will operate, thus providing the necessary guidance for policymaking by the director and staff. Policies adopted autonomously by the director and staff must be consistent with, or subordinate to, policies adopted by the board.

2. Carrying out policy is a shared responsibility of the staff, the director, and the board. The primary responsibility for implementation lies with the director. Wherever possible, the trustees must delegate responsibility for carrying out policy, but certain tasks and decisions (e.g., the solicitation of funds, the selection of the director) cannot be avoided. Furthermore, to limit the trustees' functions to policy *formulation* would exclude one of their most critical but least used prerogatives: *monitoring* the execution of policy. For example, if the director and the staff have been discriminating against women in staff employment for years, a new, explicit policy of non-discrimination is unlikely to be enforced unless the board monitors implementation thoroughly and regularly.

3. The appropriate, proportionate shares of responsibility for policymaking and for implementation among trustees, director, and staff will vary by size and type of organization. In large, complex organizations, the depth and experience of professional staff usually permits certain levels of policy to be delegated from board to director that would not be feasible in a small organization. Public organizations will differ from private organizations to the extent to which policy constraints are imposed by external bodies.

4. Although the board must not delegate its responsibility to *make* **policy in fundamental matters, wherever possible the director and staff should be encouraged to exercise the initiative in** *formulating* **policy statements for board considera-**

tion. In this way, the crucial leadership role of the director is not compromised. Equally important, the prospects for support of board policies are significantly enhanced if the director and staff have contributed to policy formulation.

The director and staff have a special role in helping the board to understand the separation of policy and implementation as it currently exists in the organization and in making informed recommendations regarding whether or not change is warranted. If the board and staff feel that change would be advisable, they must hold discussions with selected board members (chosen by the chairman), with board committees (usually the executive committee), or with the entire board. Such a self-assessment every five or ten years is a healthy means of determining whether changes in roles and responsibilities among board, director, and staff are appropriate.

Singular Responsibility for Operations

The second key organization principle is the need to assign specific responsibilities to individual members of the senior staff. Each of these individuals, all of whom are responsible to the director (as designated in the organization chart), should be given exclusive responsibility for a specific program or support service. Each person so designated directs staff in the delivery of services and provides leadership on a full-time basis. This both establishes accountability and assures that all of the organization's activities are assigned to individual staff members. Further, it provides a fundamental management device for monitoring progress and evaluating the performance of subordinates.

Assignment of Key Senior Staff

In making key assignments, the director must be cognizant of the experience, background, and strengths and weaknesses of the senior staff. The ability to direct and work with others (staff and volunteers) is extremely important. Above all, however, a positive attitude on the part of senior staff toward the organization, colleagues, subordinates, and work is essential to building an effective organization. Once assignments have been made, the director must see that senior staff members manage their particular activities in a manner consistent with the technical, programmatic, philosophical, and legal parameters developed by the board of trustees and its executive committee.

Accountability and the Balance Between Authority and Responsibility

Each position in an organization should be well-defined to establish accountability. Clear and concise position descriptions define major operating responsibilities and expected results as well as identify reporting relationships. Such descriptions promote effective operations by minimizing duplication of effort and enabling the director to hold personnel accountable for results.

Equally important is the balance between responsibility and authority. Individuals who have been assigned responsibility must have the authority to use the organization's resources to achieve objectives. Sufficient authority is necessary so that senior staff can control their own destinies.

Span of Control

This organization principle assumes that a manager can effectively supervise only a limited number of personnel. Various circumstances can determine the appropriate span of control. For instance, if job functions are similar, the number of people supervised should increase. As positions supervised become more diverse and complex, the number of personnel supervised should decrease to allow sufficient time and coverage for supervision and guidance.

Although some maintain that the number of individuals supervised should not exceed six, obviously there is no absolute limit. Whatever the number, the point is that span of control, like the other principles mentioned here, should be reconsidered periodically to determine if adjustments are required.

KEY FACTORS WHICH AFFECT THE APPLICATION OF ORGANIZATION PRINCIPLES

The organization principles just described determine how policy and operations will be separated, who will be assigned responsibility, how responsibility and authority will be divided, and what a reasonable span of control should be for the organization. There are, however, key factors which shape how these principles will be applied to meet the peculiarities of a particular arts organization.

Such factors must be identified and analyzed carefully in deciding how to organize best. The principal key factors are:

1. **Management style.** A director with a highly autocratic management style would retain much of the policymaking authority in his own office. With a decentralized style, a director would delegate policymaking to subordinates within pre-defined parameters.

2. **People resources.** The number of people available and their strengths and weaknesses should influence greatly organization structure, how assignments are made, and what responsibilities and authorities are assigned.

3. **Audience.** Should the organization's structure be modified to simplify the delivery of services or to provide improved access to the organization's constituency? Should a museum, for example, organize itself according to the types or periods of art it holds in its collection, or by programs and shows, or by some combination thereof? When combined with other independent variables, the consideration of audience needs has a great deal to do with assessing the organization's ability to accomplish its mission, goals, and objectives. Effectively organizing the art and the people responsible for it so that audience

needs are satisfactorily met will—to a large extent—determine whether the arts institution is successful.
4. **Tradition.** The historical structure, commitments, and activities that have become part of the culture of the arts organization have a strong influence on any future changes in the organization's structure.
5. **Plans.** Plans calling for changes in organizational attitudes, programs, and services often require structural change.

ORGANIZATIONAL STRUCTURE

By carefully considering the organization principles just described, and the key factors which affect them, an appropriate structure for an arts organization can be determined. The six major alternative organization structures are the functional, program, audience, geographic, process, and matrix.

Functional Structure

A functional approach to organization attempts to place people with similar skills, training, and interests in individual departments. Thus, each department is primarily concerned with its own core program or support objectives, specialists are centralized, and staff members become highly proficient in their department's function. Under this approach, all program design and delivery activities would be consolidated in one organizational entity while most support services, such as facilities management, printing, publicity, security, and crating and uncrating exhibits, would be provided by departments specializing in these services (see Exhibit 14).

One of the problems with this approach is that conflict and friction can develop among departments as each strives to achieve its own end. Frequently, as the number of programs increases, so do the difficulties inherent in specialization, such as access and equal service. Obviously, a primary difficulty in functional organizations is that the clusters of specialized personnel may not work effectively in the best interests of the total organization. Often, however, functional organizations do provide such services as publicity and security more efficiently and with better technical quality than if they were decentralized, as in the program approach.

Program Structure

In the program approach to organization, as shown in Exhibit 15, all or most services are decentralized to primary programs. Often, larger arts organizations with diversified programs and many markets are organized in this manner. Under this scheme, certain support functions, such as publicity, may be decentralized either totally or partially to the program level.

The intent of the program approach is to move control over certain services closer to the ultimate user, thereby improving responsiveness and increasing user satisfaction. However, the administrative costs of operating each division as an independent, full-service organization, coupled with

EXHIBIT 14
Henrik Arts Center
Functional Structure

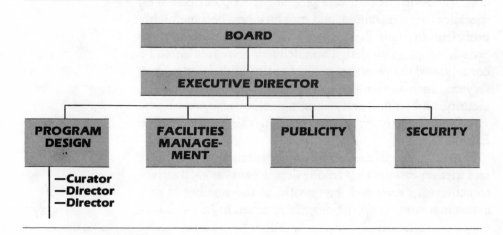

the expense of overlapping functions, can offset the anticipated benefits from improved services.

Audience Structure

If the needs of various types of audiences are appreciably
different, an organization may set up separate departments
to serve each constituency (Exhibit 16). When staffs special-
ize according to audience type, each department knows all
the facets of its audience and is well aware of constituent
needs.

With this type of structure, however, multiple audiences
create a demand for multiple organizational units. This in
turn often creates the need for different art, produced by
different means and with different standards. Responding to
many differences can move an arts organization into new
areas which are away from its central mission, goals, and
objectives. Futher, it is likely that the cost associated with
this type of structure would be prohibitive. Perhaps the old
adage, "It is impossible for a man to be all things to all people," is as true of arts organizations as of individuals.

EXHIBIT 15
Henrik Arts Center
Program Structure

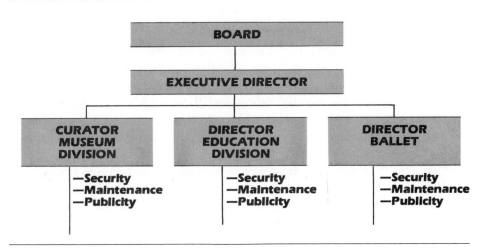

EXHIBIT 16
Henrik Arts Center
Audience Structure

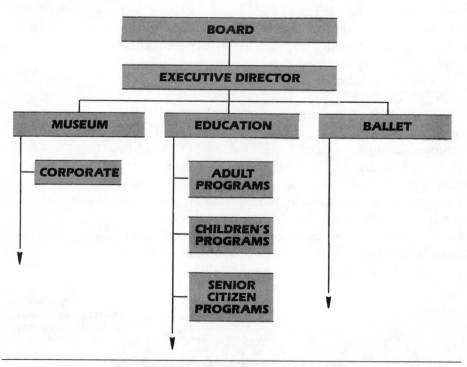

Geographic Structure

In general, the geographic approach (Exhibit 17) to structuring an organization is often most peculiar to national arts organizations—both those with a central headquarters overseeing regional offices and those which comprise regional arts organizations affiliated on the basis of common objectives. The major benefit of a geographic structure is the ability to get results because of proximity and sensitivity to local conditions. However, as with program-structured groups, individual departments in geographically structured organizations may ignore what is good for the organization as a whole and put their own goals first.

EXHIBIT 17
Henrik Arts Center
Geographic Structure

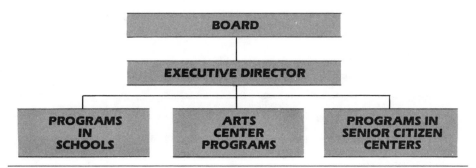

Process Structure

In the process approach shown in Exhibit 18, certain repetitive activities within a single organization are centralized. For example, rather than have separate typists for the various senior and professional staff members, the entire organization might utilize the services of a single typing pool. The main advantage of the process group is that each unit has its team of specialists. The word-processing employee is a highly specialized individual whose energy, enthusiasm, and work-time are spent on that activity without a great deal of concern about the next stage in the process.

The process approach is not limited to clerical functions, however. Setting up a long-range planning group, for example, is really setting up a process group.

Matrix Structure

In most organizations, there are multiple needs which the organization's structure must accommodate. Thus, seldom is any single structure operative in a "pure" sense. Rather, there will be a combination. The matrix structure is a means of organizing various skills, locations, experiences, and other characteristics attributable to people in an enterprise so that the most appropriate personnel are applied to meeting

EXHIBIT 18
Henrik Arts Center
Process Structure

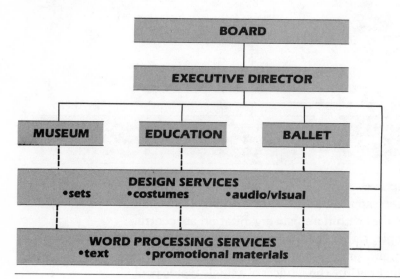

defined organizational needs. The matrix organization, as
the name implies, promotes flexibility in meeting *changing*
needs. Because it is such an important means of organizing,
the matrix structure is discussed in more detail than the
other alternatives.

For many years, arts organizations have attempted to coordinate work across established organizational and hierarchical boundaries. Along with collecting nasty comments
from staff about coordinating committees, task forces, staff
coordinators, and program managers, arts organizations have
also achieved a fair degree of success by using these devices.
Some innovative arts organizations have used these experiences as a basis for organizing program divisions, operating
departments, and even reorganizing the entire organization
in a matrix type of structure.

Many directors define a matrix structure as an organizational device that coordinates work across service boun-

EXHIBIT 19
Henrik Arts Center
Matrix Structure

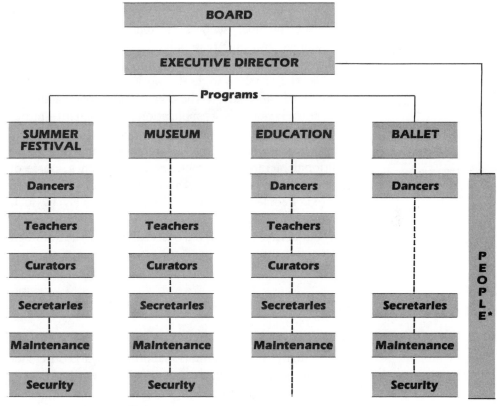

*People assignments change based on need.

daries, and thereby allows peers to work together on a collegial basis (Exhibit 19). For example, an arts and crafts museum that is organized by type of program (weaving, pottery, folk dance, and so forth) may conclude that a regional summer festival is an overriding program warranting the combined efforts of the entire museum. In such a case, a single individual—from the staff or from outside the organization—might be appointed responsible for the summer festival. Directors of each program would then relate directly to the summer festival director, who would coordinate their individual activities for the presentation of a consolidated program.

Matrix organizations basically derive from the idea that a senior staff member, such as the summer festival director, may achieve and may reasonably be held accountable for results even though he or she does not have supervisory control over the people who do the work.

The matrix approach to the organization of arts activities is not entirely new, but its application to permanent—rather than merely to temporary—work or projects *is* relatively recent. Because it is sharply different in several ways from traditional hierarchical structures, it has been a source of some irritation to staff because of the regular change required. People often initially react negatively to such changes. Yet, because it appears to offer many organizations a way out of new as well as old quandaries, it has also aroused considerable interest.

DETERMINING ORGANIZATION STRUCTURE

Selecting the appropriate organization structure is dependent on many of the organizational principles and other factors mentioned earlier. Each arts entity is presently following some form of organization philosophy. Change should be considered only if what is currently in place is not working. A new structure—following the philosophy of one or more of the structures just described—should be considered to obtain the best that is offered from each. In the end, organization structure is really a representation of how people will work together. Therefore, any structure must continually be adjusted to help people perform most efficiently and effectively.

It is important to remember that, fundamentally, it is the director's responsibility to set up a division of activities that provides the greatest advantages of specialization, facilitates control, aids coordination, ensures adequate attention to important activities, recognizes local conditions, develops people, and balances costs with benefits. In most cases, the structure he or she designs will be a mix of the approaches discussed above.

JOB DESCRIPTIONS

Regardless of the type of organization structure, it is essential that people—directors, assistant directors, curators and other staff—have a complete understanding of their roles and responsibilities. One important way to do this is to prepare written job descriptions.

The use of well-prepared job descriptions is important in establishing and dividing responsibilities and authorities. As additional people are hired, the separation of responsibility becomes more pronounced. Since this gives responsibilities and authorities to more individuals, there is greater need for clearer definitions of the role and responsibilities of each position.

A job description should provide a full understanding of the content and objectives of a job by defining and clarifying its responsibilities, authority, and accountability, as well as the way it relates to other positions.

Job descriptions are useful in several important ways:
- They help those responsible to analyze and improve organizational structure by highlighting gaps and overlaps in responsibility and authority;
- They define the relationships between individuals and within and among departments;
- They help management and staff to understand the tasks to be performed—which is essential in setting work priorities;
- They specify the knowledge, training, education, skills, and aptitudes required for the job;

- They provide a basis for formally measuring performance and for maintaining an equitable compensation program. A job description usually contains four major elements:

Description of Function. This summarizes the general function of the job and its basic objectives. It should also describe the outstanding elements that distinguish the position from others.

Specification of Responsibility and Authority. This indicates the major, specific responsibilities assigned to the position and, in most cases, designates the necessary authority. The description of responsibilities specifies standards against which performance can be measured and appraised.

Description of Relationships. This indicates the major relationships within the line of authority and at levels outside the line of authority.

Determination of Accountability. With clearly established job objectives, and well-defined responsibilities and authorities, the individual filling the position is responsible for his or her achievement. The specific standards which will be used for measuring performance should be clearly delineated. In this way, performance can be measured and appraised fairly, against standards expressed in budgets and program statements.

A job description by itself is not a panacea. It must be used by an organization for it to be effective. Thus, when hiring, the job description should be used to assess the qualifications of prospective employees. It is important that, once hired, accountability objectives be developed with the incumbent and that periodically—usually annually—performance be reviewed in light of the job description. Where appropriate, the job description should be modified to consider appropriate changes in role and responsibility. Thus, the job description is a living document which is integral to the organizational organism in carrying out its purposes. Exhibit 20 shows a sample position description for the director of the Henrik Arts Center.

STAFFING THE FINANCIAL FUNCTION

For a financial department to be effective, responsibilities should be adequately segregated. Not only does this assure that the workload is equitably shared, but segregation further provides an effective system of checks and balances to assure that responsibilities are carried out as intended. Effective segregation of responsibilities also provides vital safeguards over the use of an arts organization's precious financial assets.

Effective financial management requires detailed definition and documentation of financial activities. Segregation of responsibilities is accomplished by assigning responsibilities to specific individuals. Such assignments should be formalized by preparing written job descriptions for individual staff positions, as discussed in the previous section.

Organizations should analyze their current financial structure by noting and formally assigning financial activities to the persons presently responsible. Activities that are not presently performed should be reviewed carefully to determine how they should be assigned and executed.

Role of Key Participants

The key participants in the financial management process are the board of trustees, the director, and the chief financial officer. Assuming that an organization develops its financial management activities along the lines described in this book, responsibilities will most likely be assigned to the key participants in the following manner:

The board of trustees has an oversight and fiduciary responsibility to safeguard organizational assets. In order to fulfill

EXHIBIT 20
Henrik Arts Center Position Description

DIRECTOR

Description of Function: Responsible for directing the Arts Center activities according to policies established by the board within the resources available.

Specification of Responsibility and Authority:
- Maintains, establishes, and eliminates programs of the Arts Center with the approval of the board.
- Prepares long-range plans describing operating directions and capital needs.
- Prepares annual operating and capital budgets.
- Presents long-range plans and budgets and recommendations to the board for review and approval.
- Presents financial reports to the board periodically describing performance.
- Hires and dismisses employees based on approved funding and personnel policies appearing in the approved budget and personnel manual.
- Maintains appropriate internal controls to safeguard Arts Center assets.
- Leads fundraising activity with the support of the board.

Description of Relationships:
- Serves at the pleasure of the board.
- Reports all matters of policy to the board or its appropriate committees with recommendations for action.
- Directs the activities of all staff and is responsible for their evaluation of performance and development.
- Represents the Arts Center in matters affecting city, state, and federal government and other external bodies.

Measures of Accountability:
- Increase participation of the community in Arts Center programs (8% per year).
- Increase external funding from all sources (10% per year).
- Submit plans, budgets and periodic reports on time as established at the beginning of each fiscal year.
- Maintain a balanced budget each year with a planned surplus when possible.
- Accomplish objectives established in the annual budget.

this responsibility, the board must receive sufficient financial and related information from the director. With this material in hand, the board can establish policy and approve the plan and budget, monitor progress, and independently evaluate the financial health and results of operations of the organization.

The director is responsible for making resource allocation decisions regarding organizational operations in light of policies established by the board. In addition, the director provides the trustees with the financial management information which will assist them in fulfilling their own responsibilities. To provide this information, the director requires the support and assistance of the chief financial officer.

The chief financial officer is responsible for establishing the financial activities referred to earlier. One of the most important responsibilities is to provide the financial and related information required by the director so that he or she will be able to fulfill management responsibilities and see that board policy is carried out. The chief financial officer is also responsible for guiding the actions of subordinates and assuring the technical accuracy and integrity of accumulated information.

Qualifications of Chief Financial Officer

In selecting candidates, the organization should look for:
- Appropriate experience and training (Often, the officer is a certified public accountant and/or has a master's degree in business or arts administration. Experience in directing the financial activities of arts organizations is also important);
- Reliability and initiative;
- Understanding of both the fundamentals and the applications of fund accounting and related systems and procedures;

- Ability and willingness to assume other administrative tasks as needed;
- Ability to explain to staff and trustees the financial condition and financial performance of the organization; and
- Appreciation for the value to the community of the programs offered by the organization.

Even the best candidates may not possess all the desired qualities. In that case, the most desirable candidate is the one whose deficiencies can be most readily compensated for by other staff members or trustees.

BOARD COMMITTEES

To fulfill its many diverse responsibilities more efficiently, the board of trustees should consider establishing a committee system whereby certain activities can be delegated to selected trustees. The committee system allows the board to use the talents of individual board members based upon particular areas of expertise or personal likes and dislikes. However, ultimate responsibility for all major committee recommendations rests with the entire board. New or revised policy recommendations should first be studied by the appropriate committee and then presented for the consideration of the full board at the next regular board meeting.

The sections that follow describe the financial management role of certain committees that might be established by the board of trustees. (In certain cases, it may be appropriate to combine these activities into a single committee to better utilize the skills and time available to board members.) A more extensive treatment is given to the finance committee, where more responsibility for financial matters typically resides.

Finance Committee

The finance committee reviews and evaluates the financial reports disseminated by the organization. The committee discusses with the director the adequacy of the statements, the financial health of the organization, and plans for the future. Frequently, one individual on the board is elected as treasurer of the organization, and in some cases, the treasurer chairs the finance committee.

Presented below are the major areas in which the finance committee should become actively involved:

Planning. The finance committee should review and participate in the development of the organization's long-range plan (three to five years). Certain key questions that should be addressed include: What is the organization's purpose and programmatic plan? What are the organization's abilities, particularly in light of perceived financial strengths and weaknesses and assumptions about the future? What are the financial risks and likely results of the alternative future plans of action being considered, and can the organization afford them?

Budgeting. The finance committee must understand the activities, functions, and operations represented in the proposed budget and be able to objectively evaluate, critique, revamp, and finally, approve the budget—and the financial projections it contains.

Monitoring. In summary fashion, the committee should monitor the budget and the organization's financial status, based on periodic reports and statements from management (including balance sheets, budget-to-actual comparisons, and cash projections). The committee should review these reports in order to determine management's effectiveness in planning, controlling, and reporting operating results to date.

Budget modifications. The budget, as approved, represents board policy; therefore, any proposed changes in the budget should be reviewed and approved by the board before implementation. Based on certain established criteria, management's requests for budget modification should be submitted to the finance committee, whose role is to review requests and evaluate their probable impact on operations and the organization's financial status, and to recommend to the full board whether or not modifications are warranted.

Cash management. The committee should study the organization's cash needs and use to evaluate whether cash will be available when needed for operations and to assess whether idle cash is being invested for optimal return.

External independent auditors. The committee should retain an independent audit firm to perform the annual examination of the organization's financial statements.

Audit program. With the auditors, the committee should review each year the audit program and the approach planned for conducting the organization's next audit.

Audit results and auditor's management letter. At the conclusion of the audit, the committee should review the financial statements and the results of the audit with the auditors and management. Additionally, a management letter describing weaknesses in internal controls and other observations warranting improvement should be presented and discussed and a plan of action developed for correcting noted deficiencies.

Investment Committee

The investment committee establishes investment policy for the organization's assets. These assets include certain restricted and unrestricted funds which may become available from time to time for investment purposes. Investment policy should be based upon the interpretation of both the current and long-term financial needs of the organization.

Budget Committee

The budget committee, where it is constituted separately from the finance committee, establishes budget guidelines in concert with the director. In carrying out its role, the committee may wish to appraise the adequacy of the organization's budget development and budget administration efforts. The committee may seek to ensure that budgets are assigned at an appropriate department or division level (to establish budget accountability). Finally, the full board should approve the organization's budget as submitted by the budget committee, and ask questions and request modifications when appropriate, prior to giving its approval.

Audit Committee

The audit committee has oversight responsibility for ensuring the effectiveness of the organization's audit activities. These include internal audits performed by the internal audit department serving the organization, external audits conducted by independent certified public accountants, and audits conducted by federal auditors. The audit committee reviews the findings of external auditors and may wish to consult directly with the senior member of the audit team. This committee should also monitor the plans and evaluate the activities of the organization's internal audit department.

CONCLUSION

Organization is an essential element in the process of achieving results. The key participants in an arts organization—the board, the director, the staff—all have important roles to play in moving the organization from concept to achievement. This chapter presents certain key general principles of organization that should be helpful in structuring the organization to maximize the strengths and minimize the weaknesses of people. The implications of effective organization principles on financial management are many. There is a need to define carefully financial activities to assure adequate assignment of responsibilities to those having authority to achieve the results desired.

Organization structure should be fluid and thereby change as conditions change. Most importantly, if one structure is not working effectively, it is useful to make adjustments that might improve overall performance.

6

The Financial Management Information System

THE PRIMARY PURPOSE of a financial management information system (FMIS) is to provide the board and senior
management with timely, accurate, and relevant financial
information that will assist in the management process (i.e.,
planning and budgeting, implementing, controlling, and
evaluating). The FMIS, and the information it produces, are
essential if management and board members are to function
as informed decisionmakers.

A schematic of an FMIS and its relationship to two other
key systems that exist in every arts organization is presented
in Exhibit 21. First, at the lowest level, an arts organization
maintains an operating system, composed of various individual systems (budgeting, accounting, payroll, purchasing, fundraising, membership, and accounts receivable) each

of which has its own unique purpose, i.e., paying bills, writing payroll checks, and keeping track of individual amounts pledged by donors or due from third parties for services rendered. In addition, these systems contain important information which, when summarized and combined with

EXHIBIT 21
Overview of the Financial Management
Information System

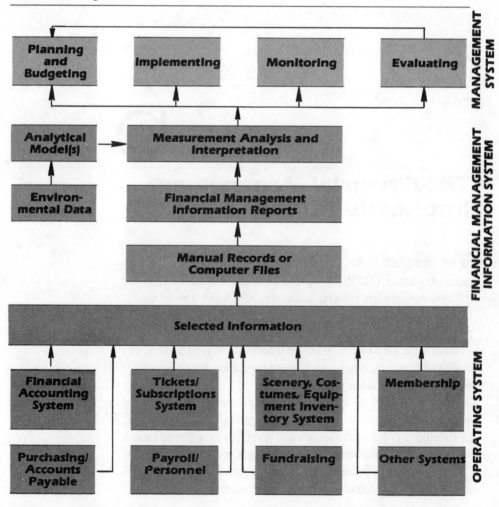

information from other operating systems, provide essential financial information for the arts manager and board of directors. At the next level is the financial management information system (FMIS), where this information is collected, combined, and then considered in the context of certain external environmental information (national and regional economic trends) which is pertinent for analysis and planning. For analytical purposes, various models are used to combine the information gathered in the FMIS.

At the highest level of an organization is the management system, which comprises planning and budgeting, implementing, controlling, and evaluating. Each of these functions, performed by management, is supported by the information that must be provided. One or more qualified individuals should be assigned the responsibility of collecting and maintaining the financial and related statistical information required. Responsibilities include conducting financial analyses, examining trends, performing comparisons to budget, and preparing and issuing reports.

FUNDAMENTAL CONCERNS

In developing an effective FMIS, one must assure that the information it provides will satisfy user needs and is timely, accurate, and consistent with prior reporting periods.
- **Relevance.** In an arts organization, the primary user of the information provided by an FMIS is the director, or chief operating officer, who needs the information to assess current financial status, past performance, and projections of future results. Similarly, the governing board must receive sufficient information so that they can advise and counsel senior management, set policy, monitor implementation, and evaluate the results.

  Senior management is responsible for ensuring that the components of the FMIS are in place and that the information provided is relevant and satisfies the needs of the board and the director. Senior management must also obtain the financial and statistical information they need to carry out their own responsibilities. The financial officer should provide assistance in defining user needs and in setting up effective systems for providing the required information.

- **Timeliness.** Financial information presented one, two, or three months after the reporting date is not useful to management. Therefore, it is essential that information requirements be clearly defined and that the FMIS be designed to produce information shortly (five to ten working days) after the end of each month.

- **Accuracy.** The financial officer of the organization must assure that reports submitted to management and to the board accurately represent operating results and the organization's current financial status.

- **Consistency.** Financial reports should conform with generally accepted accounting principles and be presented consistently from report to report. The format must be consistent in order to allow comparisons with prior reporting periods and to highlight changes which may require further analysis and attention.

REPORTING VARIABLES

The chief financial officer of an arts organization is typically the designer of financial management reports. Advice regarding information needs should be obtained from the director, other members of senior management, and the board.

In developing reports, there are two sets of variables—dependent and independent—which must be considered by the designer when determining the contours of the reported information. Organization structure, management style, and external influences (government regulations, for example) are referred to as independent variables because they are beyond the direct control of the designer of financial reports.

The dependent variables, over which the designer *does* exercise control, are form, content, frequency, and distribution.

Dependent Variables

There are only four dependent variables which must be considered in designing a financial reporting system:

1. **Form.** The structure of the report, the definition of the columns, rows, and cumulative totals of financial information;
2. **Content.** The appropriate level of detail and the scope of the information;
3. **Frequency.** How often a financial report is to be prepared (monthly or quarterly is required in most cases for financial reports covering the entire organization; daily or weekly reporting may be required for individual segments of the organization, such as a gift shop);
4. **Distribution.** Who should receive the reports (general distribution throughout the organization is not appropriate for all reports).

These dependent variables allow an enormous amount of flexibility in the design of an organization's financial reports. When the system is first designed, they are established by the designer of the FMIS to satisfy the special needs of the user of the information. Subsequently, the designer will change report frequency, content, etc., depending on the unique independent variables or needs of the organization. Thus, the dependent variables are adjusted over time to recognize the changing independent conditions occurring in an arts organization.

Independent Variables

Independent variables are beyond the FMIS designer's control. They are influenced by the cultural and operating characteristics of the organization. Thus, the number and nature of independent variables is unique to each organization, and management must make certain that each is taken into account in determining the information required.

EXHIBIT 22
Financial Management Information System
Reporting Hierarchy

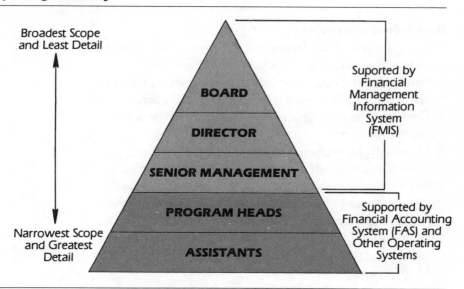

Broadest Scope
and Least Detail

Suported by
Financial
Management
Information
System
(FMIS)

BOARD

DIRECTOR

SENIOR MANAGEMENT

PROGRAM HEADS

ASSISTANTS

Narrowest Scope
and Greatest
Detail

Supported by
Financial Accounting
System (FAS) and
Other Operating
Systems

Only in this way can the designers of financial reports respond effectively to user needs. The following are some of the independent variables which are often encountered.

Responsibility Structure. Typically, arts organizations are structured hierarchically, as illustrated in Exhibit 22. Within the reporting structure, program heads or managers who are responsible for program services require financial reports representing the budget areas of their responsibilities. Accordingly, they require reports containing an enormous amount of detail but with a limited scope, focusing exclusively on their specific area of activity. In contrast, the board, director, and senior management most often require less detail, but the information must have a much broader scope since their responsibilities encompass the entire organization, or at least broader segments of the organization. As a result, reports will vary in form and content depending on the level and the responsibilities of the individual receiving them. This concept is often referred to as HIERARCHICAL REPORTING.

Clearly, an organization's responsibility structure has a substantial impact on the dependent variables of content and distribution.

Management Style. The manner in which management directs organizational activities plays an important role in financial reporting. The more participative the management style, the more likely the need to share information among those involved in organizational decisionmaking. Conversely, in an organization where decisionmaking is more centralized, the need for shared information decreases. Management style largely determines the independent variables of content, frequency, and most importantly, the distribution of information throughout the organization.

Volatility. The volatility of an organization's operations, or any of its segments, has an enormous impact on the frequency of reporting to concerned users. For most organizations that are in reasonably good financial shape, reporting monthly is acceptable. For fragile organizations, however, weekly or even daily reports on certain programs (e.g., publications or membership) may be required. For certain activities (e.g., gift shops, bookstores, and other retail operations), more frequent reporting may be necessitated by rapid changes in volume demand. This is especially true of food services because food prices are highly volatile.

External Influences. All four dependent variables—form, content, frequency, and distribution—are affected by certain external regulations and agencies. As mentioned earlier, arts organizations must comply with external regulations and with the practices and requirements of third parties that provide funds. For example, certain reports must be prepared for the federal government, state government, foundations, and the like. Similarly, an organization's basic annual financial statements should be prepared according to the generally accepted accounting principles (GAAP). (These accounting principles are described in more detail in Chapter 7.)

Certainly, there are other independent variables that influence reporting, and each organization must identify its own in order to determine what information is required to support the financial management function.

REPORTING CONCEPTS

Apart from the independent and dependent reporting variables, there are a number of reporting concepts which should be considered when designing an FMIS. These key reporting concepts are useful in helping the user—management or board—to focus on both positive and negative areas that warrant attention and, possibly, decisionmaking.

Comparative Reporting

This method of reporting allows the reader to study current financial information in the context of comparable data from the organization's prior year, from the current budget, or from similar organizations.

1. **Prior Year.** Comparing current financial information with actual results from the same period of the previous year allows the user to make informed judgments regarding the organization's current level of performance. In order to make such comparisons, the information must be prepared, from one accounting period to the next, using consistent accounting principles and practices.

2. **Budget Expectations and Actual Experience.** A budget is a financial representation of how an arts organization's resources are to be used. The budget—once established—should be the primary device used to monitor progress during the year and to evaluate performance once the year is completed. Comparison of the budget to actual exper-

ience is an important control tool which should be used by all managers.

3. **Similar Organizations.** In addition to comparing organizational results to budget or to previous years, it may be useful for management to compare an arts organization's performance with that of similar organizations. Initial comparisons often only highlight the differences, but this will allow board and management to determine if further analysis and explanation are warranted. Frequently, such comparative analyses raise questions about possible alternative policies or operating procedures which might be considered for adoption.

Some of the more commonly available sources of information on various kinds of arts organizations are: cooperative interchange of published audited financial statements among selected similar organizations; financial reports maintained by state agencies responsible for collecting and analyzing such information; and published research studies or data maintained by private organizations serving the arts.

Trend Analysis

Trend analysis involves the collection and analysis of information over time, such as a period of several years. Trend reporting is particularly useful in indicating changes in financial activity from one year to the next. It also helps put into perspective any distortions which may have been created by unusual circumstances during a particular year.

The information may be presented numerically in typical financial statement format, or it may appear in the form of charts and graphs. The latter are useful because they quickly reveal important positive and negative trends which may need immediate attention.

Exception Reporting

Exception reporting focuses senior management and board attention on areas requiring immediate attention. Thus, recipients receive key information concerning only those situations in which actual results of operations vary significantly from what was expected.

The definition of key information may vary among different organizations. For example, an organization with unusually high utility bills resulting from a large special exhibition might highlight the increased energy costs and explain to the reader the cause—and temporary nature—of the increase.

Some managers and board members are not comfortable with this approach; because of their particular management style, they prefer to review the entire organization. For such individuals, exception reporting would be unacceptable.

TYPES OF FINANCIAL MANAGEMENT REPORTS

For arts organizations, there are three types of financial reports which should be in place: (1) the basic financial statements required for top-level, internal summary reporting needs, which should conform with external reporting standards and generally accepted accounting principles (basic financial statements may also be used externally to satisfy the reporting requirements of foundations, banks, state agencies, etc.); (2) summary management reports for use by the board, the director, and senior management; and (3) analytical reports specifically designed by management to provide further information regarding elements contained in the summary reports.

Basic Financial Statements

The FMIS should routinely produce an arts organization's basic financial statements. These consist of the following:
1. Balance sheet;
2. Statement of activity; and
3. Notes to financial statements, which summarize significant

accounting policies and explain certain key financial information for the reader.

Prepared according to the accounting principles referred to in the next chapter, these basic financial statements should present all the activities for which an arts organization is fiscally responsible. They must be prepared at least annually, at the end of the fiscal year, but it is recommended that they also be prepared on a monthly basis. This will help to ensure that:

- The current status of the organization's assets and liabilities can be determined;
- Key accounting controls such as reconciliations are operating on a current basis; and
- Changes in fund balances can be monitored on a timely basis.

Full disclosure in the form of notes to the financial statements is not normally required monthly. In addition, it may not be feasible to record certain accounting adjustments such as accruals and deferrals on a monthly basis. A more detailed discussion of the basic financial statements is contained in Chapter 7.

Summary Management Reports

As mentioned earlier, financial management is an ongoing process in which managers continually examine their performance and consider changes in their activities. Frequently, important management decisions must be made relatively quickly. This requires summary management reports which present financial and related statistical information in more detail than the basic financial statements. Such reports, prepared monthly, should focus on the areas of responsibility of the organization's senior management. The structure of these reports differs from that of the reports required by managers at the department level. Summary reports are typically generated by the financial accounting system and other operating systems, as shown earlier in Exhibit 21.

EXHIBIT 23
Henrik Arts Center
Illustrative Analysis of Reports

TYPES OF REPORTS	Distribution — BOARD	DIRECTOR	SENIOR MANAGEMENT	CURATORS	FUNDRAISING DIRECTOR	MUSEUM SHOP DIRECTOR	CHIEF FINANCIAL OFFICER	Frequency — ANNUAL	QUARTERLY	MONTHLY	DAILY	SCOPE	CONTENT
1. Summary Budget Status Report	✔	✔					✔			✔		Total arts center	Budget compared to actual and outstanding encumbrances with projections to year end
2. Departmental Summary Report			✔				✔			✔		Total for each major segment of museum division	Budget compared to actual and outstanding encumbrances
3. Annual Giving Report	✔	✔			✔		✔	✔[1]				Total arts center	Budget vs. actual and pledged by
4. Membership Report	✔	✔			✔		✔		✔[2]			Total arts center	Members by type and division affiliation
5. Museum Shop Sales Report						✔	✔			✔		Museum shop	Sales by category
6. . . .													
7. . . .													
8. . . .													

1) monthly for last 3 months of year.
2) presented quarterly to the board.

Depending on the independent variables discussed earlier in this chapter, there are a number of different kinds of management reports that might be needed by the senior management of an arts organization. An illustrative analysis of the types of reports is presented in Exhibit 23, which describes the distribution, frequency, scope, and content of reports for the Henrik Arts Center. Such an analysis should be prepared for every arts organization to assess gaps and overlaps of reporting as related to the needs of key users. Selected examples of report formats are provided in Exhibit 24. The reader should be aware that all the reports referred to in the exhibits are for illustrative purposes; where appropriate, they must be adapted to the specific circumstances of individual arts organizations.

Ideally, senior management should receive financial statements monthly. If cash availability is a concern, information regarding cash position and a cash flow analysis may be required more frequently (weekly or even daily). The board's finance committee should receive financial information from management at every committee meeting. Typically, a finance committee meets quarterly. The committee, or a subcommittee, may meet more often (every two months or monthly during certain periods of the year, such as during the budget preparation cycle) if the arts organization has financial difficulties. An organization with a fragile financial condition may require this more intensive participation

EXHIBIT 24
Henrik Arts Center
Selected Examples of Report Formats

HENRIK ARTS CENTER

| | | Summary Budget Status Report
as of _____ | | | | REPORT 1 |
Budget Unit	Approved Budget	Actual	Outstand- ing encum- brances	Net Re- maining	Projection to Year End	Expected Variances at Yr. End

Department Summary Report
as of _____

REPORT 2

Budget	Approved Budget	Actual	Outstanding encumbrances	Net Remaining	Notes

Annual Giving Report
as of _____

REPORT 3

Source	Budget	Actual Receipts	Amts. Rec'd Over/(Under) Budget	Pledges Received
Individual—Annual Giving				
Corporations				
Foundations				
Memberships				

Membership Report
as of _____

REPORT 4

Types	Budget		Actual		Variance Over (Under) Budget
	No.	Amount	No.	Amount	
Museum Division					
•Corporate					
•Club					
•Individual					
Ballet Division					

Museum Sales
as of _____

REPORT 5

Category	Budget	Actual	Variance
•Pottery			
•Macrame			
•Weaving			
•Posters			
•Books			

until finances are improved. (It should be noted that if there is no finance committee, this board review function may be performed by the board of trustees, the chairman, the executive committee, or some other designee of the board.) Information submitted to the board should be current as of the end of the most recent reporting period.

Analytical Reports

When users of financial management reports identify variances from budget, unexpected results, or other indications of unusual circumstances, they frequently require further information to assist in understanding the underlying causes of these conditions. In such cases, they then should request that analytical reports be prepared to explain the circumstances behind the amounts presented. Frequently, statistical information (such as number of members at the beginning of the period, new members, renewals, members lost, and members at the end of the reporting period) is required to assist in this analysis.

CONCLUSION

The FMIS is the foundation upon which effective financial management practice is established. The FMIS should be like a central nervous system for the arts organization—telling the board, senior management, and others how things are going and when change may be necessary. The continuing need for informed decisionmaking is implicit in the management process. The FMIS is an essential source of the information which makes this possible.

An effective FMIS requires two key elements: first, a carefully designed system that considers the diverse needs of the multiple users of the information that will be provided, and second, a sound foundation of operating systems which can keep track of day-to-day events (transactions) and report progress in a timely and accurate manner.

The financial accounting system, a key operating system, is at the hub of the informational wheel, collecting in summary form all of an arts organization's financial transactions. The next chapter describes the financial accounting practices and principles that should be in place to feed information to the FMIS.

7

Fund Accounting, Accounting Principles, and the Accounting System

UNLIKE BUSINESSES ORGANIZED FOR PROFIT, nonprofit organizations receive gifts, grants, and legacies to support their activities. Often, these contributions are for specific purposes, and the organization must give assurance to trustees, donors, or other external parties that funds were spent, or preserved, according to the purposes for which they were given. Accordingly, nonprofit organizations and their accountants have developed a method of accounting, called fund accounting, especially designed to address the uniqueness of such organizations.*

*Specific needs and reporting requirements for nonprofit organizations are detailed in "Statement of Position 78-10," *Accounting Principles and Reporting Practices for Certain Nonprofit Organizations*. This book was issued by the Accounting Standards

FUND ACCOUNTING

Fund accounting is a procedure by which, for accounting and reporting purposes, resources are classified into funds associated with specific activities or objectives. Each fund is a separate accounting entity with a self-balancing set of accounts to record assets, liabilities, fund balances, and changes in fund balances. Although an organization may have many funds, separate accounts are maintained for each fund to ensure compliance with limitations and restrictions placed on the use of resources.

The fundamental principle in fund accounting is stewardship: accountability for the receipt and use of resources. Funds are accounted for separately according to restrictions established by donors or other third parties. Unrestricted funds may be designated for a special purpose by formal action of the organization's governing board. As will be shown later, the external reporting requirements in audited financial statements, nonprofit tax returns, and the like differ somewhat in each case. Nonetheless, in each case, an organization's management has a fiduciary responsibility to utilize the funds according to the stipulated conditions of third parties or the governing board. Fund accounting permits an institution to record, classify, summarize, and report financial transactions in a manner consistent with the purposes for which the funds were originally established.

FUND GROUPS

The number of different funds which an organization may have can be quite large. This depends on the number and frequency of various limitations placed on the funds, as well as on the amount of diversity in the programs carried out by the

Division of the American Institute of Certified Public Accountants. It was subsequently included, and given further accounting stature, as an audit guide, which was also published by the Institute.

organization. It has become common practice, therefore, to classify funds with like characteristics into fund groups. Each fund group is treated as a separate entity with self-balancing assets, liabilities, and fund balances. Within each fund group, separate accounting is made for individual funds—each having its own assets, liabilities, and fund balance.

The fund groups most frequently found in arts organizations are:

- Operating funds (restricted and unrestricted),
- Endowment funds, and
- Plant funds.

Operating Funds

In most arts organizations, the vast majority of financial transactions reflect the conduct of everyday operations or activities. The fund group used to account for these activities is known as the operating (or current) funds group. Funds in this group may be either restricted or unrestricted.

UNRESTRICTED FUNDS have no external restrictions on their use; they can be used for any purpose designated by the governing board. Funds received for services rendered, membership dues, and contributions, as well as other contributions to support the general purposes of the organization, would be included in this operating funds-unrestricted funds group.

In situations where the board decides to set aside certain resources for specific operating purposes, such resources are still identified as unrestricted funds, since there is no *external* restriction on use. At its own discretion, the board can reverse its previous designation, and these funds would again become available for general operating purposes. In effect, when the board chooses to set aside certain resources, they have established a DESIGNATION (or preference) for how they plan to use unrestricted funds. For accounting purposes, this becomes a subset of the unrestricted fund; it should *never* be treated as a restricted fund.

RESTRICTED FUNDS are funds whose use is restricted to

specific purposes by outside third parties. A restriction is communicated to the organization in writing and signed by the donor. Funds may also be restricted by the manner in which the organization solicits them, e.g., through an appeal letter clearly identifying the specific purpose of the contribution being sought.

Endowment Funds

Endowment funds are those for which the donor has stipulated that the principal is to be inviolate and to remain in perpetuity. The income from investment of the principal may be expended, but this must be done according to the wishes of the donor. Depending upon the donor's intent, this income may be restricted for a specific purpose or be available for the unrestricted use of the organization.

TERM ENDOWMENT FUNDS are funds that have the same characteristics as an endowment fund, except that at a specified future date or event the principal is no longer required to be maintained as an endowment. For example, a donor may specify that the principal of the term endowment shall be retained inviolate for twenty years, after which it may be used at the discretion of the board. For the first twenty years after accepting such a gift, the principal would be recorded within the endowment fund group on the organization's financial statements. Subsequently (i.e., after twenty years), these funds would become part of the organization's available operating funds, and their use could be determined internally by the board.

QUASI-ENDOWMENT FUNDS are those which the governing board, rather than a donor or outside agency, has determined through board action are to be retained and invested. The governing board has the right to reverse its action and expend the principal of these funds at its discretion. Funds in this category are sometimes referred to as "funds functioning as endowment" since, in the true legal and accounting sense, they do not meet the perpetuity tests for a "true" endowment.

Plant Funds

Plant funds are used to account for the land, buildings, and equipment owned by the organization. This group subdivides into unexpended plant funds and net investment in plant.

UNEXPENDED PLANT FUNDS are monies contributed to the organization, or transferred by appropriate board designation, for the purpose of acquiring land, buildings, or equipment. The assets of this fund, typically cash and investments, are in effect "waiting to be used." Once the necessary purchases take place, the newly acquired property is transferred to "net investment in plant."

NET INVESTMENT IN PLANT represents the total carrying value of all property, plant, and equipment. Assets contained in this fund are frequently referred to as "fixed assets" by the business community.

ACCOUNTING PRINCIPLES

The fund accounting structure, discussed earlier in some detail, is based on accounting principles unique to nonprofits. There are also many accounting principles which are followed by both nonprofit organizations and for-profit corporations. Commonly known as "generally accepted accounting principles" (GAAP), they represent those methods and conventions of recording and reporting financial information which result in a fair presentation of financial position and results of operation. Adoption of these principles allows for analysis of financial statements and comparison to the financial information of similar organizations.

Accrual Accounting

The accrual method of accounting recognizes revenues when earned and expenditures when materials and services are received. This contrasts with the cash basis of accounting, whereby revenues are recognized when cash is received and expenditures when disbursements are made. The distinction between these methods can be demonstrated by the folowing hypothetical example. Assume that the Henrik Arts Center has purchased $5,000 worth of materials to restore and rehabilitate certain of its museum pieces. The materials have been received, but Henrik has not yet paid the vendor. Under the accrual method, the receipt of materials and the related liability would be recognized within Henrik's financial statements. However, under the cash basis method, there would be no accounting transaction recorded until the materials have been paid for.

Unlike the accrual method, the cash basis of accounting does not present financial information in conformity with generally accepted accounting principles because it does not reflect a true picture of economic events. Statements prepared in this manner are much less complete and more prone to manipulation. It is therefore recommended that arts organizations adhere to the accrual method when reporting financial information.

Depreciation Accounting

Depreciation accounting is a method of distributing the cost of tangible, exhaustible capital assets (i.e., buildings and equipment) over the estimated useful life of the asset in a systematic and rational manner. It is a process of allocation, not valuation. In other words, the actual cost of an asset is allocated over its estimated useful life. There is no attempt to continuously re-value assets based upon some measure, such as replacement cost. Nonexhaustible assets—works of art and historical treasures, for example—need not be depreciated.

Double Entry Accounting

This principle recognizes the basic accounting equation that organizational assets minus liabilities equal equities or ownership (fund balance in the case of nonprofits). In other words, one side of the equation (equities) assigns a dollar value to ownership, while the other side (assets) defines the specific tangibles owned. An accounting system should be designed to recognize the effect of financial transactions on existing assets and equities. Therefore, each financial transaction requires a two-sided entry. An increase in assets will have a corresponding increase in liabilities or fund balances. For example, upon receipt of a $100 contribution, the asset (cash) increases; at the same time, overall equity also increases by the same $100. In the case of the Henrik Arts Center, if the organization purchases a new building, there will be an increase in the assets of its plant funds. At the same time, either Henrik's liabilities would increase (to indicate the need to pay for the building) or its net investment in plant-fund balance would increase by the amount or value of ownership (to indicate that the building was paid for).

In a nonprofit environment, it is also important to remember that the accounting equation remains intact by individual fund within a fund group. As discussed earlier, by definition, each fund is a *self-balancing* set of accounts in which assets less liabilities equal fund balance. Therefore, if the assets of one fund are temporarily used to pay the obligations of another fund, for accounting purposes one fund has lent assets to the other. The lender would reflect the transaction as a receivable (due from borrower), and the borrowing fund would reflect the same circumstance as a payable (due to the lender).

DESIGN CONSIDERATIONS OF AN ACCOUNTING SYSTEM

The diverse uses of financial information require that an organization's accounting system be designed to meet the needs and objectives of many different users. Confusion and misunderstanding frequently arise from the failure to distinguish between the information needs of managers and of external parties (i.e., government, funding sources).

All too often, accounting systems are developed that organize, classify, and report financial transactions to meet reporting requirements for stewardship fashioned by external requirements without fully considering the needs of management. Unlike the public accounting profession's orientation toward external reporting of expenditures by function, organizations manage their day-to-day operations by controllable budgets assigned to individuals with authority to make decisions on spending the funds. Consequently, management's need to control the use of budgeted resources should be a primary consideration in the design of an arts organization's accounting system. In particular, the fund accounting system should be equipped to provide the information needed to highlight budget variances requiring management attention. Therefore, each organization must analyze all of its information needs—both internal and external—to determine how best to organize its accounting system.

CHART OF ACCOUNTS FOR FUND ACCOUNTING

The chart of accounts is the fundamental structure through which financial data is collected. It will contain assets, liabilities, and fund balances, as well as revenue and expenditure accounts.

A nonprofit organization should carefully design its chart of accounts in order to facilitate accounting for the receipt and use of both restricted and internally designated funds. Further,the chart of accounts should:
1. Reflect the structure and activities of the organization as it presently exists;
2. Be flexible in design in order to readily accommodate future organizational shifts or changes;
3. Facilitate the systematic and well-planned collection of data;

4. Adequately describe accounts used to record financial transactions;
5. Allow for the analysis of the organization's financial activities; and
6. Permit expansion by the organization as necessary.

Typically, the chart comprises the following components: an account code structure, a listing of accounts, and account code definitions.

Account Code Structure

An account code structure describes the basic framework of accounts used by an organization to record financial transactions. Specific accounts are established in the books of account based upon this coding structure.

For example, the Henrik Arts Center might have an account code structure divided into three segments. Segment one could be used to identify major fund groups such as operating funds, endowment funds, and plant funds. Segment two would be used to identify major account classifications in two categories: organization unit responsible (e.g., exhibition department) and subfund (e.g., a grant for a special exhibition). Segment three would identify specific account classifications. These might include the type of asset or liability (cash, accounts payable), the specific revenue type (tuition/class fees, admission/ticket sales, fees/commissions, etc.), or the object of expenditure (salaries, fees, telephone, etc.). Exhibit 25 shows the basic account code structure for the chart of accounts.

Listing of Accounts

The applicability of each segment of the account code structure to a particular organization will depend upon characteristics of organizational activities. The combination of each of the three segments described above results in a listing of accounts that are to be used. Exhibit 26 shows a partial account code listing for the Henrik Arts Center.

EXHIBIT 25
Account Code Structure

A basic Account Code Structure would be:

$$X-YYyy-ZZ$$

Where: X equals Fund Groups
Y equals Account Classifications
Z equals Type of Asset, Liability, Revenue, or Expense

X may be:
1 for Operating Funds
2 for Endowment Funds
3 for Plant Funds

Y may be segregated into two groupings with the following meaning:
YY for the Organization Unit Responsible (99 organization units possible)
yy for the Individual Fund (99 funds possible for each organization unit)
Note: For a small arts organization, this second element of the code structure could be reduced to two digits, one for organization unit (Y) and one for the individual fund (y).

Z may be:
1 to 99 for a specific type of account distinguished above.

For example, if we assume that cash in First National Bank is owned by the plant fund, and that its assigned value for "Z" is 01, the full account code would be as follows:

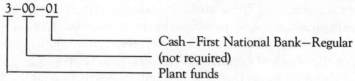

3—00—01

Cash—First National Bank—Regular
(not required)
Plant funds

If we further assumed a payment for legal fees (Z=17) out of operating funds the correct account code would be:

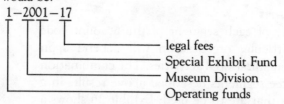

1—2001—17

legal fees
Special Exhibit Fund
Museum Division
Operating funds

The Listing of Accounts is then developed by preparing a detailed list of all of the potential digit combinations which will be used by the organization.

EXHIBIT 26
Henrik Arts Center
Account Code Listing

OPERATING FUNDS (1)

Assets (01–29)	account number
Cash: First National Bank—Regular	1-0000-01
First National Bank—Payroll	1-0000-02
First National Bank—Savings	1-0000-03
Time Deposits	1-0000-07
Accounts Receivable—School Programs	1-0000-10
—Students Tuition	1-0000-11
—Membership Dues	1-0000-12

•

Restricted Funds

Special Exhibit Fund	1-2001-00
Crafts Program Support	1-2002-00
State Council Exhibit Grant	1-2003-00

Museum Division (20)

Personnel	1-2000-01
Advertising	1-2000-06
Computer Service	1-2000-07
Conservation	1-2000-09
Consultant/Artist Fees	1-2000-12

EXHIBIT 27
Henrik Arts Center
Account Code Definitions

Accounts Receivable—School Programs   **1-0000-10**

This account is increased for all amounts billed (debits) to schools for programs in dance, crafts, etc. conducted at school sites or at the Arts Center for the benefit of schools. This account is decreased for payments or other credits received from schools. A debit balance represents amounts due from schools to Henrik.

Accounts Receivable—Crafts Student Tuition   **1-0000-11**

This account is increased by all amounts billed to students attending Crafts Council programs. This account is decreased for payments or other credits received from students. A debit balance represents amounts due from students to Henrik.

Accounts Receivable—Membership Dues   **1-0000-12**

This account is increased. . . .

Account Code Definitions

Definitions of each account contained in the chart of accounts assist users in understanding the meaning and usage of the accounts contained therein. This helps to ensure the uniform classification of financial transactions. For example, the Henrik Arts Center may have several types of accounts generically defined as accounts receivable. Within the chart of accounts, and the accompanying definitions, there would be a more specific definition of what type of receivable belongs in what account (for example, as shown in Exhibit 27, receivables due for school programs in Account 1-0000-10, receivables due for crafts student tuition in Account 1-0000-11).

THE ACCOUNTING SYSTEM

An organization's accounting system comprises three major activities: data gathering, processing and recordkeeping, and financial reporting. An overview of the typical accounting system that details each of these activities is shown in Exhibit 28.

Data Gathering/Source Documents

All the financial data that need to be gathered for the accounting system are the result of either cash receipts transactions, payroll transactions, cash disbursement transactions (other than payroll), and other accounting transactions (generally referred to as "journal entries"). For each of these four kinds of transactions, a separate accounting document should be in place for gathering appropriate data. The four basic accounting documents are the cash receipts journal, payroll records, the cash disbursements journal, and the general journal.

All cash received by an organization should be recorded in the CASH RECEIPTS JOURNAL (Exhibit 29). This document is often referred to as one of the "books of original entry," since

EXHIBIT 28
Overview of a Typical
Accounting System

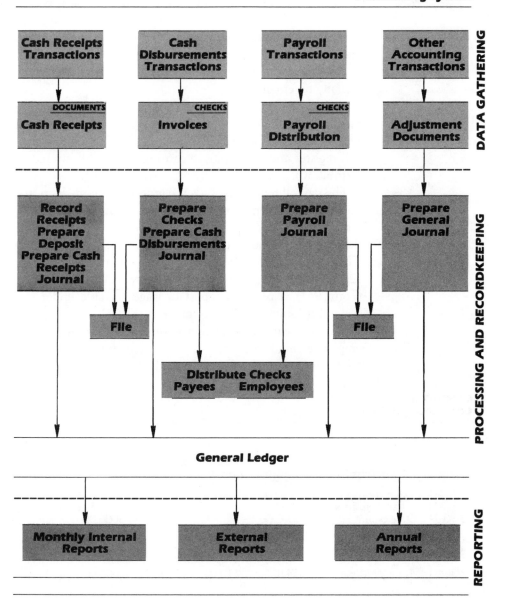

it is one of several original sources of data which is subsequently posted into the general ledger. The cash receipts journal should be updated frequently and summarized monthly. This monthly summary is typically what is posted into the general ledger. Consistent with the double entry principle previously discussed, every transaction recorded in the cash receipts journal represents an increase in the cash account(s) and a corresponding increase in another account (usually revenue).

PAYROLL RECORDS ensure that employees are paid properly and that an accurate accounting is made of earnings and taxes withheld. The required payroll records include a payroll register and an employee earnings record (illustrated in Exhibit 30).

The payroll register records the gross amount, deductions, and net pay given to each employee during a pay period. This register is designed to facilitate the calculation of deductions and the determination of net amounts to be paid. The payroll register also provides the detail needed for filing reports such as the Employer's Quarterly Federal Tax Return (Form 941), a required report of wages taxable under the Federal Insurance Contributions Act (FICA).

Employee earnings records are prepared separately for each employee paid by the organization. Each record summarizes all payments made to an individual employee during a

EXHIBIT 29
Cash Receipts Journal

		DR	CR			
Date	**Description**	**Amount**	**Member Contrib.**	**Member Dues**	**Gov't. Grant**	**Other**
3/01/84	Dave Johnson	$ 250.00	100.00	150.00		
3/16/84	Susan Tomlinson	150.00		150.00		
3/30/84	State of N.Y. (Unrestricted Support to Arts)	5000.00			5000.00	
3/30/84	John Josephs	10.00	10.00			
3/30/84	Total for Month	$5410.00	110.00	300.00	5000.00	

EXHIBIT 30
Payroll Records

PAYROLL REGISTER

Date	Name	Check No.	Hours	Rate	Gross Pay	FICA	Fed. Tax	State Tax	Insur.	Other	Net
3/01/84	Fred Potter	4615	—	—	$1500.00	120.00	300.00	160.00	19.00	—	901.00
	Joyce Stevens	4616	—	—	750.00	60.00	119.00	66.00	12.00	—	493.00
					$2250.00	180.00	419.00	226.00	31.00		1394.00

EMPLOYEE EARNINGS RECORD

Employee Name: Fred Potter
Soc. Sec. No.: 197-23-1234
Dependents: 3
Employment date: July 1, 1973
Address: 21 Sunshine Lane
Upstate, NY 11325

Date	Check No.	Hours	Rate	Gross Pay	FICA	Federal Tax	State Tax	Insur.	Other	Net
3/01/84	4615	—	—	$1500.00	120.00	300.00	160.00	19.00	—	901.00
3/15/84	4623	—	—	1500.00	120.00	300.00	160.00	19.00	—	901.00

EXHIBIT 31
Cash Disbursements Journal

			CR					DR			
Date	No.	Description	Amount	Exp. Func.	Educa-tion	Exhibi-tions	Ballet	Crafts	Gen'l & Admin.	Fund Raising
3/07/84	2507	Dave's Exterminating	$ 350.00	19	—	—	—	—	350.00	—
3/20/84	2508	N.Y. Telephone	171.18	14	—	—	—	—	171.18	—
3/20/84	2509	Tom Davis	200.00	13	200.00	—	—	—	—	—
3/24/84	2510	Ace Supplies	1,027.20	22	171.20	171.20	171.20	171.20	171.20	171.20
3/28/84	2511	Mailing List Svcs Inc.	400.00	28	—	—	—	—	—	400.00
TOTAL FOR MONTH			$2,148.38		371.20	171.20	171.20	171.20	692.38	571.20

particular year. This can be contrasted to the payroll register which summarizes similar information for all employees by pay period.

THE CASH DISBURSEMENTS JOURNAL (Exhibit 31). All cash disbursed by an organization should be recorded in this journal. (Even payroll is frequently funded by transferring money from the general disbursement account to the payroll account.) Another "book of original entry," the cash disbursements journal should be updated frequently and summarized on a monthly basis for posting in the general ledger. Typical information provided for each transaction would include: disbursement date, payee, check amount and number, and identification of the particular program the disbursement supports. Once again, each transaction is self-balancing in that for every disbursement there will be a decrease in cash and an increase in a corresponding expenditure account.

Certain accounting transactions are the result of neither cash receipts nor cash disbursements. Such transactions are called journal entries and should be recorded in the GENERAL JOURNAL. Example entries include the recording of depreciation expense and correction of entries previously made in the cash receipts or cash disbursements journals. Of course, as shown in Exhibit 32, each journal entry should be self-balancing and include an appropriate description of the rationale for the entry.

Processing and Recordkeeping

Each of the above source documents requires its own unique processing routine. For example, cash receipts transactions require the recording of receipts, the preparation of deposit tickets, and posting in the cash receipts journal. Ultimately, however, each of the source documents generates postings into the GENERAL LEDGER.

The overall purpose of the general ledger is to serve as the repository—in summary fashion—of all the organization's accounting transactions. Typically on a monthly basis,

EXHIBIT 32
General Journal

Date	No.	Description	Account No.	DR.	CR.
3/12/84	118	Education—Consultants	1-2001-13	$300.00	
		Management—Other	1-2001-28		$300.00

To correct for February disbursement no. 2502 to Maurice Long erroneously charged to Management.

transactions which had originally been recorded in the "books of original entry" are summarized and recorded in the general ledger, where a separate section is maintained for each account appearing in the chart of accounts. Accounts should be kept up to date by recording the summarized amounts from the books of original entry at the end of each month. When the recording process in the general ledger is completed, accounts should be added to ensure that the cumulative amounts of debits is equal to the cumulative amount of all credits. This is referred to as preparing a TRIAL BALANCE of the general ledger.

The general ledger, as shown in Exhibit 33, is the one document which contains, in summary form, all types of accounting transactions. Thus the various reports needed by an organization can be obtained by using this ledger. Information on assets, liabilities, revenues, and expenses are all recorded within this document.

FINANCIAL REPORTING

Reports derived from the general ledger and the books of original entry are prepared to assist management and the board in meeting their respective responsibilities for controlling resources, evaluating the results of previous decisions, and planning and budgeting for future needs. Reports may be financial (e.g., dollars collected) or statistical (e.g., patrons served). For purposes of this book, we are focusing

EXHIBIT 33
General Ledger—Sample Pages

Henrik Arts Center

Account Title: Regular Checking   **No.** 11

Date	Description	Ref.	DR.	CR.	Balance
2/28/84	Balance Forward				$17,001.26
3/31/84	March Receipts	CR-9		5,410.00	
3/31/84	March Disbursements	CD-9	2,148.38		$13,739.64

Account Title: Education   **No.** 51

Date	Description	Ref.	Total	Salaries & Wages	Consult-ants	Supplies
—	Balance Forward	—	$112,000.00	91,000.00	6,300.00	14,700.00
3/31/84	March Disburse.	CD-9	371.20	—	200.00	171.20
3/31/84	General Journal	GJ-9	300.00	—	300.00	—
			$112,671.20	91,000.00	6,800.00	14,871.20

on financial reporting, although the reader may find many of the reporting techniques appropriate for statistical reports.

Financial reports serve a variety of purposes. Some satisfy internal management needs, others meet external reporting requirements, while still others might be useful for both. In the following sections, the basic financial statements which should be prepared by an arts organization will be discussed as well as some basic principles which should be followed to ensure adequate report preparation. The basic financial statements represent the minimum level of financial reports that an arts organization will need to produce if it is to follow generally accepted accounting principles.

Basic Financial Statements

An arts organization's basic financial statements, including related footnotes (see Notes to the Financial Statements below), are the balance sheet and the statement of activity. These are the reports which are typically prepared to fulfill external reporting requirements.

The BALANCE SHEET (see Exhibit 37 on page 182) presents the financial status of an institution—its assets, liabilities, and the fund balances for each fund group—at a particular point in time. The balance sheet is a "snapshot" of financial position as of the date of the report. Unlike the statement of activity, the balance sheet is static (i.e., it reports as of a point in time rather than through a period of time). This report enables the reader to readily compare one point (this year) to another point (last year at the same time).

The STATEMENT OF ACTIVITY (see Exhibit 36 on page 180) reports the support, revenue, capital or nonexpendable additions, and program expense categories during a specific period of time (typically a fiscal year). In addition to the activity for the period, the statement should include a reconciliation between the beginning and ending fund balances, and thereby articulate with the balance sheet. In some organizations, this statement might carry a different title, such as STATEMENT OF SUPPORT, REVENUE, EXPENSE, CAPITAL ADDITIONS, AND CHANGES IN FUND BALANCES or STATEMENT OF CHANGES IN FUND BALANCES. Some organizations may prepare two statements: a statement of activity and a separate statement of changes in fund balances.

The NOTES TO THE BASIC FINANCIAL STATEMENTS (not illustrated, see AICPA audit guide for examples)—including the summary of significant accounting policies—represent an integral part of an organization's financial statements. Notes provide additional details that may be useful to the reader in understanding the financial position or the results of the organization's operations. They act as a "bridge" between the minimum requirements of the financial statements themselves and the total information that management feels is necessary in financial reports to provide the reader with an adequate understanding of the organization's financial condition.

Auditing the Basic Financial Statements

In instances where a nonprofit organization solicits contributions from the public, the organization may be required to report its activities to some regulatory agency. Such reports frequently include the organization's financial statements and a report on the statements by an independent auditor. In his report, the independent auditor renders his opinion as to whether the financial statements are presented fairly in accordance with generally accepted accounting principles.

An organization may also engage an accountant to compile or review its finanical statements. Although the scope of this work is much less than what is accomplished during a complete financial statement audit, it is still valuable to have an external authority review and comment on the organization's existing procedures in report preparation.

Finally, an organization may benefit from external assistance in tax return preparation. Although nonprofit organizations are generally exempt from paying federal and state taxes, there are certain types of transactions which might in fact be taxable. Further, exemption from tax payment should not be confused with exemption from tax filings. With the exception of very small organizations, all nonprofits need to file some sort of return with federal, state, and sometimes, city authorities. The external auditor, or representatives of federal and local tax departments, will be able to help define a particular organization's tax reporting requirements.

Accounting Principles and Financial Reporting

The accounting principles contained in this chapter describe the basic standards of accounting that are followed by arts organizations. These principles provide a common language with which to record, report, and interpret an organization's economic events. Use of this common language affords independent auditors, external agencies, trustees, and managers with the consistency of information they need to weigh confidently the financial performance and health of an arts organization for a particular reporting period and to compare it to previous reporting periods and with the financial performance of comparable organizations.

Accordingly, it is important that arts organizations prepare financial transactions and the resulting financial reports—i.e., balance sheet, statement of activity—according to these accounting principles. Accounting principles are the fundamental structure upon which all accounting and reporting is based.

8

Ratio Analysis

RATIO ANALYSIS and operational indicators can be used by arts administrators to highlight critical conditions which warrant timely management and board attention. This tool encourages positive financial conditions and provides information needed to initiate corrective actions when conditions arise that may be detrimental to the organization's future.

Ratios are indicators of financial health or distress, and ratio analysis is a shorthand method for examining an arts organization's financial position and activities. When examined over time, they indicate trends which may be positive or negative; when used in comparisons with "peer" organizations, they highlight anomolies and raise questions which may be worthy of further analysis.

Operational indicators are statistical representations of

activity used to monitor the performance of an arts organization's financial function; they may also be developed for program and other support services. Operational indicators provide detailed information about how an arts organization operates in terms of the timeliness and efficiency of its activities rather than dollars and cents.

RATIO ANALYSIS FOR THE ARTS

Arts administrators, trustees, and others are often concerned about the financial status and operations of their organizations. The financial statements which they receive are maintained according to fund accounting principles, and the information contained in these statements is sometimes difficult to assimilate. Ratio analysis is an attempt to ease the process of examining and understanding the financial activities of an arts organization.

In analyzing financial activities, users of financial statements must understand what has occurred during the past year regarding sources and uses of funds, users may need to examine other reports such as the statement of activity.

The focus of such an analysis is historical, in that users (i.e., arts administrators, board members, and others as appropriate) strive to understand the financial activities of the most recently completed fiscal year. Essentially, these individuals should be asking three fundamental historical questions about the organization:

1. Is the reporting arts organization clearly financially healthy, or not, as of the reporting date?
2. Is the reporting arts organization financially better off, or not, at the end than it was at the beginning of the year reported on?
3. Did the reporting arts organization live within its means during the year reported on?

Most financial statement users recognize that the answers to these questions are not provided in depth by ratio analysis.

Rather, the ratios are attempts to summarize the financial activities detailed in the financial reports, and they suggest other subsidiary questions that naturally follow from the summary analysis. This gives rise to the fourth fundamental historical question:

4. Why have the arts organization's financial ratios behaved in the manner observed?

Because the financial reports reflect the policy decisions made earlier by the administration and the board, the ratios help users of financial reports to understand the results of these decisions.

ASSESSMENT OF FINANCIAL CONDITION: BALANCE SHEET RATIOS

Readers of financial statements want to know the financial condition of the organization. The term "financial condition" describes the reader's interest in determining the position or status of the organization in terms of the value assigned to its available reserves. There are three major ratios of financial condition which are referred to as the balance sheet ratios: the ratio of expendable assets to total liabilities, the ratio of expendable fund balances to total expenses, and the ratio of nonexpendable fund balances to total expenses.

To illustrate these ratios, the financial statements shown in Exhibits 36 and 37 on pages 180 and 182 have been used to calculate the ratios for the Henrik Arts Center. The numbers used in the ratios, both here and throughout this chapter, can be identified by comparing the letters indicated in the ratio formulas with the corresponding letters indicated on the Henrik Arts Center's financial statements.

1. Ratio of Expendable Assets to Total Liabilities (Ratio 1).
This ratio measures the relative liquidity of the organization. It is a fundamental indicator of financial strength. The ratio is expressed as follows:

$$\frac{\text{Expendable Assets } (A)}{\text{Total Liabilities* } (B)}$$

*(exclusive of restricted, deferred amounts)

The NUMERATOR, Expendable Assets, is composed of all assets except for those of endowment funds and those already expended on land, buildings, equipment, and other fixed assets at the end of the fiscal year, as reported on the balance sheet. The DENOMINATOR, Total Liabilities, is composed of all liabilities, both current and long term.

Ratio 1 reflects the concept that one of the most basic determinants of financial strength is the availability of sufficient cash, or assets that will convert to cash in the normal course of business, to meet all obligations as they come due. Significant to the usefulness of this ratio is the condition that only expendable assets are counted. Investments in land, buildings, and equipment, while representing assets of an organization, cannot be counted in this ratio because they will not produce cash unless sold, something not normally anticipated since these assets are assumed to be needed to execute current programs. Thus, the ratio expresses the relationship between expendable assets and all liabilities.

A ratio of 1:1 or greater indicates that there are more current assets available than current liabilities. Accordingly, if an organization were to settle its accounts at the balance sheet date, it would be able to pay all liabilities, while if a ratio of less than 1:1 is experienced, the converse would be true. Ratios of 0.3:1 or less may indicate that an organization is experiencing cash flow difficulties.

For the Henrik Arts Center, the ratio would be as follows:

Henrik Arts Center

CURRENT YEAR	PRIOR YEAR
$\dfrac{\$645,500}{\$319,900} = 2.02$	$\dfrac{\$893,000}{\$386,000} = 2.31$

In this example, it appears that the liquidity of Henrik Arts Center is twice as strong as the 1:1 threshold referred to earlier. Of concern, however, is that liquidity has declined since the prior year. If this trend were to continue unchecked over the next few years, the Henrik Arts Center's liquidity could become impaired. Certainly, more analysis is required to assess what the financial condition is and what has transpired since last year. Although the ratio indicates strength, the absolute dollar size of expendable assets is not substantial when compared with Henrik's operating activities (discussed further in Ratio 2).

2. Ratio of Expendable Fund Balances to Total Expenses (Ratio 2). This ratio describes the organization's ability to fund current programs and other expenses from expendable fund balances should no additional operating revenues be available. This ratio is expressed as follows:

$$\frac{\text{Expendable Fund Balances } (C)}{\text{Total Expenses } (D)}$$

The NUMERATOR, Expendable Fund Balances, is composed of unrestricted, unappropriated funds and funds designated for investment and for plant expansion. The DENOMINATOR, Total Expenses, is composed of all current programs and support expenses.

Ratio 2 is an important measure of financial strength relative to the organization's operating size. Expendable funds should increase at least in proportion to the rate of growth of operating size. If they do not, the same dollar amount of expendable funds will afford a diminishing margin of protection against adversity as an organization grows in dollar level of expenses. Such a negative trend over time indicates a weakening financial condition.

The ratio of expendable funds to total expenses serves another purpose: It acts as a check on the ratio of expendable assets to total liabilities (Ratio 1). Small amounts of expendable assets (or worse, the absence of such assets) signal a weak financial condition. A comparison of such assets to inconsequential liabilities would not necessarily produce a valid measure of liquidity. In some instances, significant liabilities do not exist. Obviously, in these cases the ratio of expendable assets to liabilities would not be useful. The ratio of expendable fund balances to total expenses would be a much more valid measure of financial strength.

No absolute value has been identified for Ratio 2 that would indicate that an organization is clearly financially healthy. Experience suggests, however, that a ratio of 0.3:1 or better would be required to reinforce significantly the ratio of expendable assets to total liabilities.

For the Henrik Arts Center, the ratio would be as follows:

Henrik Arts Center

CURRENT YEAR	PRIOR YEAR
$\dfrac{\$\ 325,000}{\$1,946,000} = .167$	$\dfrac{\$\ 507,000}{\$1,727,000} = .294$

This ratio indicates that the Henrik Arts Center's financial strength has declined from the prior year relative to its operating size. Certainly, the current year ratio is well below the 0.3:1 threshold. As was the case for Ratio 1, a continuation of this trend signals a need to focus attention on ways to reverse the trend and assure that expendable fund balances increase at least proportionately to operating size.

3. Ratio of Nonexpendable Funds to Total Expenses (Ratio 3). This ratio describes the relative strength of an organization's nonexpendable funds (sometimes referred to as capital funds) in supporting its current operating size. Capital funds are funds like endowments, whose principal cannot be expended and must be held intact in perpetuity. However, these funds do produce income. Other capital funds, such as term endowment funds, annuity and life income funds, may be converted for use by the organization at some future time. This ratio is expressed as follows:

$$\frac{\text{Nonexpendable Funds } (E)}{\text{Total Expenses } (D)}$$

The NUMERATOR, Nonexpendable Funds, is composed of endowment, term endowment, annuity, and life income fund balances as reported on the balance sheet. The DENOMINATOR, Total Expenses, is defined in the same fashion as in Ratio 2.

Ratio 3 is important because it provides an overall assessment of nonexpendable funds that in themselves are not usable for operating and plant purposes. Although the principal of nonexpendable funds must remain intact, it can still act as a significant source of financing for operating and plant requirements. For example, endowment funds produce income and capital gains which may be used for operating and plant purposes. Thus, nonexpendable funds have a current impact as well as both short- and long-term implications for the future of the organization.

Again, presently there is no reliable index to indicate how large nonexpendable funds should be. Many organizations today are concerned about the size of these funds relative to the operating size of the organization. Clearly, the higher the value of Ratio 3, the more favorable the organization's financial condition. A declining trend in this ratio probably signals a weakening financial condition, although such a conclusion requires confirmation from Ratios 1 and 2.

Henrik Arts Center

CURRENT YEAR	PRIOR YEAR
$\dfrac{\$2,900,000}{\$1,946,000} = 1.49$	$\dfrac{\$2,831,500}{\$1,727,000} = 1.64$

This ratio indicates that the Henrik Arts Center has a reasonably strong capital base which is approximately one and one-half times the size of operating expenses. Even though endowment funds have increased slightly, this strength had declined somewhat since the prior year, due to the fact that expenses have increased at a faster rate than the endowment.

EVALUATION OF FINANCIAL PERFORMANCE: NET OPERATING RATIO

The question of financial performance is a continuing interest for readers of financial reports. Reporting on financial performance involves understanding the overall net operating achievements of an organization. Such an understanding permits the reader to focus attention on the causes which produced the financial condition described earlier in the balance sheet ratios.

4. Ratio of Net Total Support and Revenue to Total Support and Revenue (Ratio 4). This ratio indicates whether total current operations of an organization for the year resulted in a surplus or deficit. This ratio provides the most succinct answer to the question: Did the reporting organization live within its means during the year being reported upon? The ratio shows the percentage of an organization's revenues which remains after operating expenses are applied. It is expressed as follows:

$$\frac{\text{Net Total Support and Revenue } (F)}{\text{Total Support and Revenue} (G)}$$

The NUMERATOR, Net Total Support and Revenue, is composed of all operating fund support and revenue, less expenses. The DENOMINATOR, Total Support and Revenue, is composed of all operating fund support and revenue.

For Henrik Arts Center, the ratio would be as follows:

Henrik Arts Center

CURRENT YEAR

$$\frac{(\$ \ 128,000)}{\$1,818,000} = -.07$$

PRIOR YEAR

$$\frac{(\$ \ 24,700)}{\$1,702,300} = -.01$$

For the Henrik Arts Center, a negative ratio has resulted, indicating that Henrik has operated at a deficit for the past two years. To continue to operate with a negative ratio will cause further erosion of the financial strength of the arts center.

EVALUATION OF FINANCIAL PERFORMANCE: CONTRIBUTION AND DEMAND RATIOS

For most arts organizations, the support and revenue from operations and related expenses represent the major sources and uses of funds. Further analysis of these support revenues by source and by program expense can also be prepared. These ratios address the fourth fundamental question that the analyst seeks to answer: Why have the organization's financial ratios behaved in the manner observed?

Contribution Ratios

CONTRIBUTION RATIOS indicate the contribution of an organization's various sources of support and revenue to the funding of its operating expenses. The contribution ratios that follow are derived from the main sources of revenue appearing on an arts organization's statement of activity:

- Ratio of Shops to Total Expenses (Ratio 5)
- Ratio of Tuition/Class Fees to Total Expenses (Ratio 6)
- Ratio of Admission/Ticket Sales to Total Expenses (Ratio 7)
- Ratio of Fees/Commissions to Total Expenses (Ratio 8)
- Ratio of Trips/Workshops to Total Expenses (Ratio 9)
- Ratio of Investments to Total Expenses (Ratio 10)
- Ratio of Other Income to Total Expenses (Ratio 11)
- Ratio of City Grants to Total Expenses (Ratio 12)
- Ratio of County Grants to Total Expenses (Ratio 13)
- Ratio of State Grants to Total Expenses (Ratio 14)
- Ratio of Federal Grants to Total Expenses (Ratio 15)

- Ratio of Private Grants to Total Expenses (Ratio 16)
- Ratio of Individuals—Annual Giving to Total Expenses (Ratio 17)
- Ratio of Corporate Foundations to Total Expenses (Ratio 18)
- Ratio of Memberships to Total Expenses (Ratio 19)
  These ratios are expressed as follows:

<u>Support and Revenue Items *(H)*</u>

Total Expenses *(D)*

The NUMERATOR is the source of income presented in the statement of activity. The numerators for the ratios just listed are for illustrative purposes. The numerators of these ratios will vary depending on the sources of revenues peculiar to each organization. The DENOMINATOR, Total Expenses, is defined as described for Ratio 2.

The contribution ratios for the Henrik Arts Center are as follows:

Henrik Arts Center

RATIO	CURRENT YEAR	PRIOR YEAR
5. Shops	$\dfrac{\$\ 101,000}{\$1,946,000} = 5.2\%$	$\dfrac{\$\ \ 80,700}{\$1,727,000} = 4.7\%$
6. Tuition/ Class Fees	$\dfrac{\$\ \ 48,300}{\$1,946,000} = 2.5\%$	$\dfrac{\$\ \ 37,800}{\$1,727,000} = 2.2\%$
7. Admissions/ Ticket Sales	$\dfrac{\$\ 172,000}{\$1,946,000} = 8.8\%$	$\dfrac{\$\ 136,700}{\$1,727,000} = 7.9\%$
8. Fees/ Commissions	$\dfrac{\$\ \ 22,000}{\$1,946,000} = 1.1\%$	$\dfrac{\$\ \ 17,600}{\$1,727,000} = 1.0\%$
9. Trips/ Workshops	$\dfrac{\$\ \ 14,400}{\$1,946,000} = 0.7\%$	$\dfrac{\$\ \ 10,900}{\$1,727,000} = 0.6\%$
10. Investments	$\dfrac{\$\ 176,500}{\$1,946,000} = 9.1\%$	$\dfrac{\$\ 178,400}{\$1,727,000} = 10.3\%$

11. Other Income	$\dfrac{\$\ 21,000}{\$1,946,000} = 1.0\%$	$\dfrac{\$\ 19,400}{\$1,727,000} = 1.1\%$
12. City	$\dfrac{\$\ 15,000}{\$1,946,000} = 0.8\%$	$\dfrac{\$\ 33,500}{\$1,727,000} = 1.9\%$
13. County	$\dfrac{\$\ 110,000}{\$1,946,000} = 5.7\%$	$\dfrac{\$\ 100,400}{\$1,727,000} = 5.8\%$
14. State	$\dfrac{\$\ 75,600}{\$1,946,000} = 3.9\%$	$\dfrac{\$\ 67,000}{\$1,727,000} = 3.9\%$
15. Federal	$\dfrac{\$\ 45,800}{\$1,946,000} = 2.4\%$	$\dfrac{\$\ 113,600}{\$1,727,000} = 6.6\%$
16. Private	$\dfrac{\$\ 34,200}{\$1,946,000} = 1.8\%$	$\dfrac{\$\ 25,500}{\$1,727,000} = 1.5\%$
17. Individuals— Annual Giving	$\dfrac{\$\ 215,000}{\$1,946,000} = 11.0\%$	$\dfrac{\$\ 195,600}{\$1,727,000} = 11.3\%$
18. Corporate Foundations	$\dfrac{\$\ 720,000}{\$1,946,000} = 37.0\%$	$\dfrac{\$\ 650,000}{\$1,727,000} = 37.6\%$
19. Memberships	$\dfrac{\$\ 47,200}{\$1,946,000} = 2.4\%$	$\dfrac{\$\ 35,200}{\$1,727,000} = 2.0\%$

The contribution ratios for the Henrik Arts Center indicate that the greatest proportion of support and revenue to fund expenses is derived from corporate foundations, individuals—annual giving, and investment income. A reduction in the proportion of support and revenue from federal grants has primarily been offset by increases in the proportion from various sources of earned income.

Demand Ratios

DEMAND RATIOS refer to program expenditures which use available revenues. The demand ratios that follow are derived from the primary and support program service expense

categories appearing on an arts organization's statement of activity:
- Ratio of Curatorial to Total Support and Revenue (Ratio 20)
- Ratio of Conservation to Total Support and Revenue (Ratio 21)
- Ratio of Exhibitions to Total Support and Revenue (Ratio 22)
- Ratio of Crafts Council to Total Support and Revenue (Ratio 23)
- Ratio of Publicity and Public Relations to Total Support and Revenue (Ratio 24)
- Ratio of Fundraising to Total Support and Revenue (Ratio 25)
- Ratio of Division Administration to Total Support and Revenue (Ratio 26)

These ratios are expressed as follows:

$$\frac{\text{Program Expense Category } (I)}{\text{Total Support and Revenue } (G)}$$

These ratios indicate the proportional demand of the various program expense categories on the total available support and revenue. They are especially useful in trend analysis to determine whether a particular category of program expenditures is receiving a growing or dwindling share of the total revenues available. The NUMERATOR is the program category of current funds expenditures. The numerators listed in the ratios above are for illustrative purposes (see Exhibit 36 on page 180). As with the contributions ratios, the numerators in the demand ratios will vary depending on the program categories defined by each organization. The DENOMINATOR, Total Support and Revenue, comprises all revenue and support from operations plus donated services, annual giving, and grants.

The demand ratios for the Henrik Arts Center are as follows:

Henrik Arts Center

RATIO	CURRENT YEAR	PRIOR YEAR
20. Curatorial	$\frac{\$\,192{,}000}{\$1{,}818{,}000} = 10.6\%$	$\frac{\$\,151{,}700}{\$1{,}702{,}300} = 8.9\%$
21. Conservation	$\frac{\$\,131{,}100}{\$1{,}818{,}000} = 7.2\%$	$\frac{\$\,124{,}400}{\$1{,}702{,}300} = 7.3\%$
22. Exhibitions	$\frac{\$\,390{,}100}{\$1{,}818{,}000} = 21.5\%$	$\frac{\$\,357{,}000}{\$1{,}702{,}300} = 21.0\%$
23. Crafts Council	$\frac{\$\,87{,}000}{\$1{,}818{,}000} = 4.8\%$	$\frac{\$\,72{,}100}{\$1{,}702{,}300} = 4.2\%$
24. Publicity and Pub. Relations	$\frac{\$\,57{,}000}{\$1{,}818{,}000} = 3.1\%$	$\frac{\$\,47{,}100}{\$1{,}702{,}300} = 2.8\%$
25. Fundraising	$\frac{\$\,47{,}000}{\$1{,}818{,}000} = 2.6\%$	$\frac{\$\,41{,}000}{\$1{,}702{,}300} = 2.4\%$
26. Division Administration	$\frac{\$\,70{,}400}{\$1{,}818{,}000} = 3.9\%$	$\frac{\$\,66{,}100}{\$1{,}702{,}300} = 3.9\%$

An examination of the demand ratios for the Henrik Arts Center indicates an increasing proportion of "demand" on available revenues in all program areas except administration. Since there are no program expense categories with a decreased "demand" on available revenues to offset the increases, it would appear that the Henrik Arts Center's expenses are increasing at a rate faster than its revenues. Clearly, there seems to be an indication of a deteriorating financial condition which calls for management's attention.

Comparisons to Other Organizations

Some arts organizations may find it useful to compare themselves to other arts organizations. These may be PEER organizations that are essentially similar in program scope and objectives, or they may be ASPIRATION organizations that the arts organization wishes to emulate. The purpose of comparisons is to raise questions regarding financial activities that are similar or different. The intent is not to suggest that an organization should replicate what others have achieved but rather to identify possible alternative directions that might be considered.

OPERATIONAL INDICATORS

Operational indicators are measures of organizational activity. They describe input, process, and output activities of key segments of an arts organization.

The Importance of Operational Indicators to the Financial Management Process

Operational indicators are statistical and financial measures used to explain the performance of programs. Principally, they involve measures of activity over a specific period of time. The intent is to highlight in a formal way financial operating conditions that are improving, staying the same, or worsening. An unimproved or worsening condition may require special attention and action.

The board of trustees and director should be concerned with operational indicators because they explain why certain changes in finances have occurred. Operational indicator reports should be prepared at least annually for the board and more frequently for the director.

Types of Indicators

Organizations should determine their information requirements by identifying departments and activities which should be monitored regularly. In making this selection, consideration should be given to the volume of transactions (such as the number of sales made in the gift shop at different times of the day or on different days of the week) as well as to the sensitivity of the activity (such as the influence of various types of exhibits or performances on buying). The paragraphs that follow discuss some common operational indicators that may be used by arts organizations. This list is not intended to be all-inclusive. Accordingly, organizations should evaluate their unique needs to identify indicators which are appropriate.

Demand for Services. One of the key operational measures involves demand for services and the concepts of quantity and quality. Of particular interest are:
- The number of attendees at exhibits and performances,
- The number of attendees who are members of the arts organization, and
- The number of attendees who participate in annual giving.

Capacity. A second key operational measure involves capacity—the ability of the arts organization to use available space effectively. Of particular interest is the percent of capacity utilized by a paying constituency (in total and on different days and times of day).

Areas Requiring Monitoring of Operational Indicators

Monitoring such key summary indicators is essential in managing financial resources effectively. Once summary indicators are identified, more detailed information by department or activity may be useful for selected areas. For instance, the following paragraphs discuss indicators which can be used in the financial area.

Accounts Payable Department. The ability to pay creditors promptly establishes credit and enables an organization to take advantage of cash discounts and to better manage existing funds. Accounts payable performance indicators which may be useful are:
- Daily/weekly number of unpaid invoices,
- Number of occurrances per week where invoices were

initially received outside the invoice processing department, and

- Number of occurrances per week in which the invoice processing department was unable to match a purchase order with the vendor's invoice and the department-approved receiving report. (This indicator is designed to measure the degree to which operating departments fail to comply with established purchasing procedures designed to properly document the receipt of goods and services.)

Payroll Department. Personnel costs are a large part of the expenditures of an organization, and the ability to promptly add employees to the payroll, or to delete them, can be critical. Prompt payment and distribution of payroll costs to department accounts is essential. Important indicators of performance in this area are:

- Average number of days from the point of new hire or change in status to add an individual to payroll or change status,
- Average number of days from the point of receipt of approved termination notice to completion of the process, and
- Frequency of payments to terminated employees.

Negative trends in these indicators will require special attention to practices and procedures in other offices, such as the personnel department or the program directors.

Program Inquiries Concerning Monthly Financial Reports. The ability of primary and support program directors to receive timely and accurate budgetary and financial information is critical to being able to manage. It is equally important that actual or perceived errors or other difficulties experienced by programs be addressed in a formal manner by accounting department personnel and resolved on a timely basis.

Large arts organizations should consider utilizing a formal FINANCIAL REPORT INQUIRY FORM for the transmittal of inquiries by programs and as a permanent record in support of adjustments or corrections made to financial reports. Important indications of performance in this area of concern are:

- A monthly status report of the number of program inquiry forms received, processed, resolved, and the number remaining unprocessed or unresolved by program departments, and
- The number of days each month required to distribute financial reports, measured from the last day of each month.

Accounting Reconciliations. The organization is required to prepare monthly key reconciliations designed to ensure accuracy and reliability of the accounting records. Important indicators include, but are not limited to, the following:

- Indication that all bank accounts are reconciled monthly,
- Indication that all subsidiary ledger balances are reconciled to general ledger balances (e.g., accounts receivable, fixed assets, travel advances, loans).

Readers interested in further information regarding operational indicators and their application should read *Reporting of Service Efforts and Accomplishments*, a research report prepared by Peat Marwick and published by the Financial Accounting Standards Board, and *Management Indicators in Nonprofit Organizations*, a research report funded and published by Peat Marwick.

9

Asset Management

HOW WELL AN ORGANIZATION manages and utilizes its assets is an important barometer of the efficiency and resourcefulness of the organization's overall financial management operation.

Assets can be broadly divided into two major categories: cash (and cash equivalents such as certificates of deposit) and fixed assets. In this chapter, both categories will be discussed, noting the general objectives and overriding concerns which apply to each. Emphasis will be placed on the cash (and cash equivalent) sections, since many organizations will have few (or no) fixed assets of significance to manage. (Also, if a few relatively simple principles are adhered to, fixed assets are generally easier to control than cash.)

CASH MANAGEMENT

Cash is a medium of exchange. It is also a measure of value. An arts organization receives cash from its members, subscribers, private donors, and government sources. This cash is used by an organization to purchase the services, materials, supplies, and equipment that it consumes when conducting programs. Cash measures the value of such purchases to an arts organization, either as assets or as expenditures incurred in conducting organizational activities.

Cash management is an integrated process consisting of three major components: accounts receivable, concentration, and accounts payable. As the name implies, the "common thread" in all cash management activities is cash. An organization receives cash as a result of efforts made during the accounts receivable process. During the concentration phase the organization assures itself, through careful planning and investment, of optimum earnings at the lowest possible cost. Finally, cash leaves the organization as a result of the accounts payable process. In the following sections, this cycle will be discussed in further detail. First, however, cash itself will be examined.

The Cash Management Process

An effective cash management system uses existing cash properly and establishes proper controls over its inflow and outflow. The overall objectives are:

- To maximize the amount of cash available for investment without a corresponding decrease in service,
- To invest available cash in a manner that will maximize investment income, and
- To provide an effective means of monitoring and evaluating the organization's cash management program.

The following sections discuss various tools and techniques that arts organizations can use to achieve these objectives.

Maximizing Available Cash

An organization committed to maximizing its available cash should be mindful of the following:

- The accessibility of cash should be limited.
- Prompt billing of receivables will expedite timely collections.
- Payments to vendors and other third parties should be made in a timely, *but not hasty*, manner.

Limiting the Accessibility of Cash

The more people who have direct access to cash and the larger the number of bank accounts used by an organization, the more difficult it will be to determine cash availability at a particular point in time. If you are unable to identify available cash, you will likewise be unable to properly invest it. Only by limiting accessibility to cash can an organization maintain the necessary control.

Contrary to this principle, many organizations maintain several cash accounts, both checking and savings. Reasons vary from a desire for decentralization to a concern that funds received as gifts from external sources and those internally designated for special purposes be segregated from general funds.

Although segregating cash in separate accounts according to specific purposes helps an organization to maintain accountability for the ultimate use of each fund, the practice is often time-consuming and results in an inability to readily determine the organization-wide cash balance at any given point in time.

To allow maximum use of cash, all funds should be deposited in a single checking account. The segregation of funds according to purpose should be accomplished through the accounting system.

Because cash is the most "liquid" of all assets, it can easily be misused or misappropriated. Therefore, an organization must establish effective controls over all cash assets. These controls include the following:

1. Dual signatures (preferably including the signature of an officer of the organization) should be required for all checks over a certain dollar amount in order to establish a formal internal check on large disbursements.
2. Check-signing authority should be limited to as few responsible individuals as possible, while still allowing for an efficient flow of work. Only personnel with a clear understanding of the responsibilities involved should be authorized to review, approve, and issue disbursements.
3. Cashiering and cash-related functions should be separated from the accounting function by having different personnel perform each function. This establishes an internal check on the use of cash assets.
4. To ensure that all cash and cash items are accounted for, the organization should conduct a periodic examination of cash funds.
5. Each month, all bank accounts should be reconciled to the accounting records of the organization. Reconciliations should be performed by someone who does not have responsibility for, or access to, cash. These reconciliations should be reviewed periodically to make certain that they have been properly prepared and to ensure that all reconciling items are correct.
6. The organization should establish a maximum on the amount of cash that may be held in petty cash or change funds at any time in order to limit exposure to theft or loss. Cash exceeding this amount must be promptly deposited in a bank.
7. All employees who perform cashiering functions should be adequately bonded to provide effective insurance coverage of loss or misappropriation of cash assets.

Additional controls may be appropriate, depending on the circumstances. Because cash is such a vulnerable asset, controls are necessary even in very small organizations.

Prompt Collection of Receivables

No matter how highly motivated, few contributors or

recipients of service send in money before they are requested to do so by an organization. Therefore, it is crucial that amounts due but unpaid be billed promptly.

Although each organization is somewhat unique, typical forms of funding include membership dues, season subscriptions, government grants, and annual campaigns. For each type of controllable revenue source, the organization needs to examine how its own actions are contributing to an effective cash management program. If, for example, annual membership dues are not requested until after the end of the current year's membership, the organization should consider pre-billing the future year a month or two in advance. Once the invoices have been sent to the membership, it is quite likely that a certain portion of those invoiced will make payment sooner than the final due date. Certainly, funds are less likely to be received late if requests are sent out early.

Organizations may also want to examine their approach to billing. Although in certain circumstances it may be entirely appropriate to bill everyone at a predetermined time—season subscribers, for example, there are other situations where a "cyclical approach" to billing might be considered appropriate for other cash management objectives. Consider, for example, the annual push to invoice all members for their membership dues. If, instead, the organization established a practice of invoicing 25 percent of its membership each quarter, a more regular, steady stream of cash would flow into the organization. Also, the work flow for an organization's accounting personnel would be distributed more evenly and follow-up on nonpaying members would be easier to perform.

Controlling Payables

In arts organizations, controlling payables is an area frequently overlooked as a method of effective cash management. Certainly, bills should be paid on time. Failure to do so leaves the organization with a bad credit rating and possibly a further reduction in cash due to the payment of finance charges. However, the organization gains nothing by paying bills too promptly. With the possible exception of vendor discounts, pre-paying invoices results in a decrease in the cash balance and a subsequent decrease in the organization's ability to generate investment income.

Maximizing Investment Income

If an organization is able to apply the concepts described in the previous section, it will then have more cash available at any given point in time than in the past. The true value of available cash derives from its ability to generate *more* cash, in the form of investment income.

Although constant changes in banking laws preclude the development of a comprehensive list of investment alternatives and their relative return, the following questions should be considered in evaluating various possibilities. First, how much cash is available for investment? Second, how long will this cash be available? Third, how much risk can an organization reasonably take when purchasing an investment vehicle?

The answer to the first question is largely mathematical. It is calculated by determining the cash on hand, adding expected inflows (receipts), and deducting anticipated outflows (disbursements) of cash.

The response to length of availability of cash—largely determined by answering the first question—will enable the organization to decide whether short-term or long-term investments are the most appropriate course of action. As the names imply, the greatest distinction between these categories is the expected duration of the investment vehicle. A SHORT-TERM INVESTMENT is typically for a period of 30 to 360 days; a LONG-TERM INVESTMENT is typically for a period of at least one year.

The question of risk is much more subjective. All organizations should establish written guidelines defining an acceptable level of risk for various investments. As a general rule, the more risk an organization is willing to assume, the higher the rate of return. There are two questions management should ask to help make this determination:

1. If cash is needed, can it be obtained without impinging upon the investments which have been made?
2. Will the organization's future be seriously affected if the investments diminish in value?

The extent to which these key questions are answered relative to future financial security will determine the amount of risk the organization can safely afford. More often than not, excess cash is usually invested in least-risk, marketable high-grade securities to assure the retention of the principal's value and access to it if required.

Short-Term Investments

Short-term investments include the following:

- **Certificates of Deposit** are instruments issued by a bank or other savings institution. They represent a stated sum of money which has been deposited in the institution for a stated period of time. The certificate also states the specific amount of interest which is to be added to the principal at maturity. These instruments are usually protected by the Federal Deposit Insurance Corporation (FDIC), thereby minimizing the risk of the investment. Early withdrawal, however, will likely result in severe interest penalties.
- **Treasury Bills/Notes and Bonds** are obligations of the United States Treasury. As such they have a high level of liquidity and a low level of risk because they are supported by the credit of the federal government. Accordingly, interest rates are lower than for other instruments.
- **Money Market Funds** are open-ended mutual funds, each comprising a pool of cash from many investors, that invest in money market instruments. These instruments include treasury bills, commercial paper, banker's acceptances, repurchase agreements, and certificates of deposit. Because a portfolio of investments is involved, the risk of

a reduced return is generally lower. This investment vehicle does not enjoy the security that is associated with federal government paper, although it is likely that a portion of a money market fund's investments will contain federal government obligations.

Short-term investments normally provide a higher rate of return than a checking or savings account. However, investments of this kind often require a minimum investment and may carry provisions prohibiting their redemption prior to maturity, or penalizing the investor by assessing a reduced interest rate should they be cashed in prior to their due date. As mentioned earlier, this higher rate of return does bring with it a higher degree of risk. Very often, acceptable levels are achieved by some combination of investment vehicles.

Long-Term Investments

The long-term investments most commonly used by arts organizations are stocks and bonds. Although the astute investment advisor may want to point out other investment vehicles (such as precious metals, coin collections, futures trading, investment property, etc.), the lengthy terms which these alternatives require, and the inherent risks involved, make it unlikely that such long-term vehicles would be appropriate for readers of this book.

When a stock is purchased, the buyer becomes a part owner of the entity issuing the stock. In addition to the value of ownership, the purchaser of stock may receive dividends declared from time to time by the entity. Consequently, the ultimate cash value of the stock will depend upon the success, or failure, of the purchased entity. Temporary peaks and valleys are often reflected in the purchase and sales price, and because fluctuations are often difficult to predict, an arts organization must exercise caution in determining both the kinds of companies to be invested in and the amount of stock to be purchased.

Unlike stocks, bonds are the liability of the selling entity.

With bonds, the seller agrees to repay the principle advanced, plus interest, over an established time period.

Investment Policy

Ultimately, the form of an organization's investments, and the degree of risk it is willing to take, will be a function of its overall investment policy, the ultimate objective of which is to generate cash. Investment policy might be to maximize income or to maximize growth, or some combination thereof. Such policy is typically established by an organization's board of directors—frequently by the finance or investment committee. Some of the primary factors which affect whether investments are made to maximize income or growth are:

- the economy,
- the investment climate,
- the conservative nature of the board, and
- the short-term need for income to support current operations.

An arts organization must strike a balance between its short-term need for cash and the opportunity to make investments which, over the long term, will increase its base of assets.

It is important to remember that investment policies should be re-evaluated on a periodic basis. As an organization matures and circumstances change, previous investment decisions may no longer be appropriate.

MONITORING AND EVALUATING
THE CASH MANAGEMENT PROGRAM

To manage cash effectively, it is necessary to determine cash position—that is, the amount of cash presently available. It is equally important to know when cash may be received or disbursed in the future. Two reports which may be used for

EXHIBIT 34
Cash Status Report

HENRIK ARTS CENTER
CASH STATUS REPORT

Date: _____

Bank Accounts	Opening Balance, 2/21/84	Deposits (Add)	Disburse- ments (Subtract)	Closing Balance, 2/28/84
1. First National Bank—Interest- Bearing Checking Acct.	$2,900	6,100[1]	6,100[1]	2,900
2. Hudson River Savings Bank— Savings Acct.	2,100	—0—	—0—	2,100
Total Cash-in-Bank	5,000	6,100	6,100	5,000 (A)

Short-Term Investments	Opening Balance	Purchases	Disposals	Closing Balance
1. Certificate of Deposit	4,000	—0—	—0—	4,000
2. Certificate of Deposit	—0—	5,000[1]	—0—	5,000
3. Money Market Funds	5,000	—0—	—0—	5,000
Total Short-Term Investments	$9,000	5,000	—0—	14,000 (B)
Cash Position (A+B=C)				19,000 (C)

1) $5,000 that won't be needed until June, converted to CD; also see $6,100 disbursement.

these purposes are the Cash Status Report and the Cash Projection Report.

The Cash Status Report

The availability of cash is determined by completing a Cash Status Report. This report may prepared daily, weekly, or monthly, depending on the timing and significance of the organization's receipts and disbursements. An example of the Cash Status Report appears as Exhibit 34. For purposes of illustration, the exhibit uses information based on our case study, the Henrik Arts Center. It lists all the organization's bank accounts and short-term investments. In separate columns, it presents the opening balance, deposits or purchases of investments, disbursements or disposals of investments for the period being reported (that is, for the day, week, or

EXHIBIT 35
Cash Projection Report

HENRIK ARTS CENTER
CASH PROJECTION REPORT

Month Beginning: 3/1/84

Description	First	Second	Third
Opening Balance	$ 5,000[1]	4,600[2]	10,800[2]
Receipts			
Shops	40,000	50,000	50,000
Tuition/Class Fees	5,000	45,000	30,000
Admission/Ticket Sales	15,000	15,000	15,000
Fees/Commissions	4,300	4,300	4,300
Trips/Workshops	0	0	0
Endowment Income	16,200	16,200	16,200
Government Grants	7,000	47,000	9,000
Individuals—Annual Giving	10,000	12,000	12,000
Corporations/Foundations	15,000	10,000	10,000
Memberships	20,000	20,000	20,000
Certificate of Deposit Due	0	4,000[3]	0
Total Receipts	132,500	223,500	166,500
Disbursements			
Personnel	100,000	115,000	115,000
Advertising	5,000	13,600	5,000
Computer Service	3,200	3,200	3,200
Consultant/Artist Fees	0	26,000	6,000
Postage	600	4,500	600
Printing	800	3,000	3,000
Security Fees	500	6,000	6,000
Supplies/Materials	10,000	6,500	10,000
Maintenance	4,000	9,800	4,000
Telephone	750	3,000	750
Gas	100	100	100
Electric	2,450	3,000	3,000
Other	5,500	23,600	6,000
Total Disbursements	132,900	217,300	162,650
Closing Balance	$ 4,600	10,800	14,650

1) Represents closing balance 2/28/84 (See Exhibit 34).
2) Represents closing balance first and second month respectively.
3) Represents certificate of deposit redeemed during month.

month), and the closing balance. If each column is added across and down, a total of available cash in the form of bank balances and short-term investments can be determined.

The Cash Projection Report

Every organization should know how much cash it will need and how much will be available in future periods. For this purpose, a Cash Projection Report should be prepared monthly, for a three-month period, and more frequently if necessary. The projections in the report reflect cash received from a variety of sources. Similarly, the purposes for which cash is to be expended during the projection period are also included.

An example of this report appears in Exhibit 35. Again, it provides typical illustrations that may be associated with the case study, the Henrik Arts Center. The projection begins with the actual balance of total cash available; this is obtained from the Cash Status Report. Expected receipts and disbursements for the month are added to this opening balance. The resulting amount is the anticipated closing balance for the month. The closing cash balance then becomes the opening balance for the succeeding month, and the projection process is repeated until all three monthly columns of the report are obtained. The completed report permits the organization to plan in advance for the most effective use of available cash or to provide for predicted cash shortages.

FIXED ASSET MANAGEMENT

Whereas the emphasis of cash management is on the ability to generate additional assets through investment, the emphasis on fixed asset management is directed toward safeguarding and preservation. This can best be understood by examining the types of assets identified in each of these broad categories. In discussing cash management, the asset categories considered were cash, accounts receivable, and investments. Within fixed asset management, the primary concerns are about land, buildings, equipment, and works of art. Due to the nature of the former category, it is much more susceptible to rapid change than the latter.

Safeguarding Fixed Assets

Because of the generally static nature of fixed assets within an arts organization, they can usually be preserved and protected by adhering to a few basic principles. These would include:

1. Maintaining a detailed inventory of fixed assets owned by the organization;
2. Assigning responsibility for specific assets to specific individuals within the organization;
3. Ascertaining that all assets are properly maintained (it generally becomes more costly to purchase new items than to maintain the ones presently owned); and
4. Making certain that all assets are adequately insured (this is particularly true for works of art that are associated with the mission of the organization).

The Fixed Asset Inventory System

To prepare a fixed asset inventory, one must first define a unit of measure. For purposes of this discussion, a fixed asset shall be defined as an item having a unit cost of at least $200 and a useful life of two years or more. Organizations may also choose to vary this definition by asset class (e.g., office equipment, art related, computer equipment, educational equipment). For example, items which can broadly be defined as "office equipment" might be included if they have a certain unit value and useful life, but all items defined as "art related" would also be counted regardless of unit value.

The next phase of an inventory system is the actual count. Each item which meets the criteria established above must be counted and identified. Specific identification methods may vary, but those most frequently employed are special inventory tags (attached to the item) or the serial numbers assigned by the manufacturer. When items are counted, the specific location (building, room, etc.) should be indicated in the inventory records. In addition, the name of the person who will be responsible for the item should also be indicated.

Once an inventory is taken, it is important to keep records up-to-date. Additions should be recorded on a timely basis. Similarly, there should be a mechanism to remove items which no longer are owned by the organization.

Maintenance requirements and insurance needs are determined by the asset management system. By identifying and assigning monetary value to inventoried items, such a system facilitates the organization's ability to provide adequate safeguards.

In conclusion, although the emphasis differs somewhat between managing cash (and related assets) and fixed assets —the former stressing control and utilization and the latter control and safeguarding, both categories have a major impact on the operations of the organization. Effective financial management cannot be limited to either category exclusively. The common thread for all asset management is control. Depending upon the nature of the asset, the prudent use or the adequate protection of assets is another key component of the effective financial managmement an organization needs to accomplish its mission.

Appendices

Appendices

Federal Grants Management

FREQUENTLY, AN ORGANIZATION finds itself seeking more and more money from its regular contributors to pay for new or expanded programs. For some arts organizations, there is a threshold of support above which even the staunchest supporters of an organization will be unwilling to go. Consequently, a variety of new funding sources should be cultivated on a regular basis, including grants from federal, state, and local government sources, and from corporations and foundations. This allows the ballet, symphony, or museum to react with flexibility to anticipated shortfalls from traditional benefactors.

Acceptance of grants from the federal government, however, obligates an arts organization to comply with important regulations on the use of funds, allowable costs that may be charged to the grants, and reporting requirements. Compliance with these regulations is essential if arts organizations are to avoid cost disallowances and discontinuance of future funding.

The purpose of this chapter is to discuss some of the advantages of using the federal government as a funding source. In addition, some of the obligations and reporting requirements that are assumed by organizations funded in this manner will be discussed.

GRANTS DEFINED

Many arts organizations seek grants from federal agencies such as the National Endowment for the Arts, the National Endowment for the Humanities, or the Institute of Museum Services. Management and the board, however, should be aware that accepting funds from governmental agencies carries with it requirements for strict accountability and for commitment of certain demands on facilities and staff.

A grant is a binding agreement that has as its purpose the transfer of money (or other value) to a recipient arts organization to accomplish a public purpose authorized by federal statute. The grant is generally written in terms which specify how the funds are to be used. Grant funds also carry certain limitations and accompanying requirements. For example, title to equipment purchased with grant monies often rests with the grantee. Unused grant funds must generally be returned to the federal government. Many grants also contain cost-sharing provisions that require the organization to incur some costs to accomplish the proposed program or activities described in the original grant proposal and subsequent award.

The cost principles associated with these agreements are found in Office of Management and Budget Circular A-122. In addition, the Uniform Administrative Requirements covering such agreements can be found in Office of Management and Budget Circular A-110. The contents of each of these documents are discussed below.

ALLOWABLE COSTS

Office of Management and Budget (OMB) Circular A-122, "Cost Principles for Nonprofit Organizations," discusses fifty selected items of cost in a section referred to as Attachment B. The purpose of the attachment is to describe those items of cost which are allowable, those which—for federal purposes—are unallowable, and those which may be allowable under certain circumstances. The circular also states that failure to find a particular item of cost in Attachment B is not intended to imply that such costs are unallowable. Determination of the allowability of these costs should be based on the treatment afforded similar items of cost. If your organization is to be the recipient of federal monies, a careful review of the circular is suggested. In some instances, it may be advisable to seek experienced, outside professional assistance.

Arts organizations should also remember that "allowability" is a federally defined concept. Certain costs which are considered unallowable for federal purposes may be considered perfectly valid business expenses by management, as well as by other funding sources, such as corporations and foundations. For example, entertainment costs as identified in A-122 are unallowable; yet, a certain amount of entertainment may be a necessary cost of doing business. It is not the government's intent to prohibit all entertainment costs, but rather to see that no entertainment costs be charged, directly or indirectly, to the federally sponsored programs.

Salaries and Wages

Charges to grants for salaries and wages, whether treated as direct or indirect costs, will be based on documented payrolls approved by a responsible official, or officials, of the organization. The distribution of salaries and wages to awards must be supported by effort reports of personnel. An effort reporting system is required to document how staff members have spent the time for which the federal government is being charged. It also supports certain indirect costs charged to the federal government through the organization's indirect cost rate.

Because it would be impractical to identify all staff time charged to grants on a continuing basis, the federal government requires employees to support their directly or indirectly charged time by using AFTER-THE-FACT reporting of their sponsored activity. Such reports should be prepared monthly and should be retained as evidence of time spent which may be referred to by federal auditors if required. Each report must account for the total activity (100 percent of the effort) for which the employee is compensated. Thus, an employee of a dance company working on a federal grant as well as other programs and administrative activities should submit a monthly report indicating the percentage of effort expended on each activity. The report must be signed by the individual employee or by a responsible supervisory official having first-hand knowledge of the activities performed by the employee.

Equipment

Items of equipment are defined in Circular A-122 as non-expendable, tangible personal property having a useful life of more than two years and an acquisition cost of $500 or more per unit. This circular, as well as Circular A-110, states that equipment and related depreciation or use charges must be supported by adequate property records and that a physical inventory must be taken at least once every two years.

Other Costs

Other costs, such as materials, supplies, and employee fringe benefits, are also allowed by the federal government. These costs are defined in OMB Circular A-122. Frequently, additional information regarding cost allowances are described in the grant award document.

Indirect Cost Recovery

The federal government, through Circular A-122, recognizes that there are certain indirect costs associated with the performance of a federally sponsored activity. The circular also describes the methodology for developing an indirect cost rate—the percent of allowable indirect costs in relation to total direct costs—to be used by the grantee in recovering an appropriate portion of indirect costs. It is important for arts organizations to be aware of their right to recover these costs. In many organizations, the careful preparation of the indirect cost rate to obtain maximum allowable recoverable costs can spell the difference between financial health and instability in the year during which federal support has been received.

In general, indirect costs are defined by the federal government as those items of cost that have been incurred for common or joint objectives and cannot be readily identified with a single cost objective, such as a federally sponsored program. An example of indirect cost is general administration, encompassing the costs associated with the director's office, the accounting and financial offices, and so forth.

Take, for example, a relatively modest award of $50,000 received by the Henrik Arts Center. If an indirect cost rate of 30 percent is assumed, an additional $15,000 could be received by Henrik from the government by performing the activities called for in the award agreement. These funds are billed and received during the grant period according to the cost reimbursement practices established by the funding agency. They are intended to reimburse the indirect costs associated with the federally sponsored activity.

ADMINISTRATIVE REQUIREMENTS AND AUDITABILITY OF COSTS

Upon the acceptance of federal funds, an arts organization agrees to comply with the requirements of the Office of

Management and Budget Circular A-110, "Grants and Agreements with Institutions of Higher Education, Hospitals, and Other Nonprofit Organizations—Uniform Administrative Requirements." The circular is separated into several attachments, each attachment addressing a particular area of concern. These include:

- cash depositories
- bonding and insurance
- retention and custodial requirement for records
- program income
- cost sharing and matching
- standards for financial management systems
- financial reporting requirements
- monitoring and reporting program performance
- payment requirements
- revision to financial plans
- closeout procedures
- suspension and termination procedures
- a standard form for applying for federal assistance
- property management standards
- procurement standards

Arts organizations which receive federal monies should become familiar with the circular and establish policies and procedures that comply with the federal regulations.

Included in the financial management systems attachment is a requirement for biannual independent audits of the organization. The purpose of the A-110 audit is stated as a "test of the fiscal integrity of financial transactions, as well as compliance with the terms and conditions of the federal grants and other agreements." The latter portion of this statement generally distinguishes the scope of the A-110 audit from that typically performed by an external independent auditor. (The A-110 audit requirement involves additional tests and certifications by the auditors. At this writing, it is being pilot tested by the government on several nonprofit organizations.)

In addition to the possibility of an organization-wide

A-110 audit, the other types of audits which could be expected to occur are as follows:

Direct Cost Audit. Federal agencies have the right to audit the direct costs charged to the federally sponsored agreement. The principle thrust of such an examination would be consideration of the allowability of costs as described in Circular A-122.

Audit of the Indirect Cost Proposal. On an annual basis, recipients of federal awards are required to submit an indirect cost proposal to support the indirect cost rate which will be applied to federally sponsored agreements. This proposal is subject to audit by the federal agencies. The objective of the federal auditors will be to determine whether the organization has conformed with the methodology and cost principles defined in Circular A-122 in the preparation of their indirect cost proposal.

Conclusion

When an arts organization receives federal funds, it accepts these funds under certain stipulations and guidelines. Two major regulations applying to arts organizations are OMB Circular A-122 and A-110. It is essential that arts organizations follow the principles and practices described in these documents to avoid cost disallowances, which require that the organization repay the federal government for funds defined as inappropriate expenditures.

B

Automating Administrative Systems

IN RECENT YEARS, much technological change has occurred in the management of information. Today, the ability to use automated means to record, process, classify, summarize, and report information is more available to arts organizations than ever before. This chapter describes selected key concepts that arts organizations should consider as they move into the computer age.

CHANGING SYSTEMS NEEDS

Arts organizations are under increasing pressure to process and retrieve more information with greater speed and efficiency. Governing boards, increasingly concerned about their fiduciary responsibilities, frequently request information to aid them in policymaking. Arts managers need timely, accurate, and detailed information to carry out their responsibilities. Government agencies and other third parties require summary information and detailed reports on program activities which they support. In addition, already difficult operational functions, such as paying, receiving, and the retention of detailed records (for membership and fundraising purposes), are becoming more complex.

One apparent solution to these increasing demands on arts organizations is to introduce new automated word and data processing systems. For those only now considering automation, the variety of hardware (micro-computers and mini-computers) currently available presents a confusing array of capabilities and prices. The relative advantages and disadvantages of various administrative system software packages (programs) merely adds to the confusion, particularly since all programs are not compatible with all computer equipment. And the constant, rapid changes in computer technology make it difficult to know the best time to purchase equipment. "Should we buy a computer today, or should we wait for the new computer with new advanced technology which is likely to be announced within the next six months, year, two years?" is a question frequently voiced even by those who are most eager to become a part of the computer age.

For those with existing computer hardware and software, other concerns are evident: Hardware may be outdated and no longer supported by the hardware vendor, and much of the software now in use was developed for the computer equipment of ten or more years ago. Many organizations have updated their hardware to current technology and modified the old software to meet changing needs, to integrate redundant data contained in separate systems, or to attempt to adapt to new technology. Yet, in spite of these modifications (in some cases because of them), many software systems are operating inefficiently. More importantly, modified software is frequently not flexible enough to satisfy changing requirements.

For arts organizations, the question of when and how to introduce or improve automated systems focuses on a number of critical choices and conditions, including: the broad, often confusing range of available hardware and software; the compatibility question; the organization's current level of automation; staff experience; and the financial and personal resources required to purchase, implement, and maintain a system. The key to solving this automation dilemma is to choose software best suited to an organization's needs and then to implement the new system successfully. But before discussing in detail the various options and advantages offered by systems automation, the administrative systems themselves must first be examined.

ADMINISTRATIVE SYSTEMS DEFINED

As discussed in earlier chapters, administrative systems generally include the following components:
- Planning and Budgeting
- General Ledger
- Cash Receipts
- Cash Disbursements
- Personnel and Payroll
- Position Control
- Purchasing
- Accounts Payable
- Ticket Control and Ticket Billing
- General Accounts Receivable
- Student Admissions and Registration
- Membership, Fundraising, and Development
- Inventory—Point of Sale for Gift Shops
- Investments
- Collection, Costume, or Set Inventory

- Work Order Accounting for Plant Operations and Maintenance
- Internal Specialized Service Facilities Charging
- Library Bibliography and Cataloguing
- Word Processing

With each of these system components, automation simplifies the manual requirements of detailed recordkeeping and permits the easy preparation of summary reports necessary for daily operating activities and long-term decisionmaking. For example, if an arts organization has a manual accounts payable/disbursements system, it is likely that they require numerous accounts payable clerks to review invoices and assure that payments have not already been made, and to prepare checks, record disbursements, prepare mailing envelopes, and perform other tasks. Such efforts are time-consuming and, for a large organization, are subject to error, potential duplicate payment, and frequent late payment as volume increases. An automated system minimizes this effort. For instance, when invoices are received, a vendor account can be readily accessed to determine if prior payment has been made; if not, a payment request can be indicated. If authorized, a check can be prepared automatically based upon approved control procedures. In addition, the payment date can be predetermined to manage cash flow and to take advantage of available discounts. Thus, bills can be paid on a timely basis while providing maximum use of cash for the arts organization.

As is clear from this one example, an effective system, if automated, can help an arts organization to significantly improve its productivity and use of resources. In fact, many organizations have discovered that additional staffing required to handle current or increasing volume can be reduced if systems are automated, thus eliminating cost.

What must be determined is whether the cost and effort associated with introducing automation are worthwhile when compared to the time and effort saved in processing transactions and to improved management control and information. As a general rule, systems with large volumes of transactions should be automated.

A system can be automated by buying commercially available software, or an organization may choose to design and program its own. For most arts organizations, however, it is better to buy a software package.

THE ADVANTAGES OF SOFTWARE PACKAGES

The process of developing computer programs in-house can be extremely laborious, and it is often difficult to attract and retain computer professionals capable of developing and maintaining a new system. Consequently, many organizations purchase commercially available software packages. The primary advantages of these packages are that:

1. The basic features of the system typically will have been tried and proven by similar organizations, thus providing the added benefits of what was learned elsewhere;
2. Standard programs and related systems documentation have already been developed and tested;
3. External professional support is available during and after implementation, as needed; and
4. Cost, in the long run, is usually substantially lower.

These advantages have markedly reduced the risks normally associated with systems development.

HARDWARE SELECTION, ACQUISITION, AND INSTALLATION

The cost of hardware is declining rapidly, and this trend is expected to continue in the near future. Still, arts organizations must be careful not to purchase hardware without first considering their software needs, the expected use of the hardware, and the memory capacity necessary to meet current and future needs.

The effectiveness of computer hardware is limited by the availability of useful—and usable—software. Too often, organizations have purchased hardware and later found that many of the programs they needed were unavailable. Because not all computer manufacturers provide software, it is essential that compatible software be found and evaluated before purchasing a computer system.

Both software documentation (technical manuals and user instruction manuals) and sufficient personnel training (on site and at the sales office, as negotiated) from the vendor are needed to insure that the staff will be able to operate the newly installed system. Vendor support during the on-site installation of hardware and software is another important consideration.

Clearly, the expected use of the hardware must be considered: the number of administrative systems, the data storage requirements for each, and the need for access to the equipment by those who will use it. For example, if data storage capacity is too small, the system may not operate efficiently and, in some cases, may not be able to execute certain computer programs, even though they are otherwise compatible with the system. Accordingly, the hardware will have to be upgraded, which costs more money and may be disruptive to the organization's operations. For this reason, system needs should be carefully planned before hardware and software commitments are made.

Once selections have been made, contract development and negotiations are conducted with the hardware and software vendors. In each case, the contract specifies the respective responsibilities of the vendor and the organization, and must be carefully negotiated to protect both parties. The contract should indicate: when the vendor will deliver and install hardware and/or software; what will be delivered; how it will be tested to assure the arts organization of satisfaction; and, in addition to the hardware and software, the various services and materials, such as training and documentation, which the vendor will provide.

IMPLEMENTATION: KEY CONCERNS

Once hardware is installed and operating, efforts shift to implementing software. Although purchasing a software package reduces systems design time and should eliminate programming responsibilities, a number of tasks are still left to the arts organization.

First, in order to get the most out of the new software, the staff must think through the organization's current operational policies and practices to determine how they might be adapted to the special features offered by the software package.

Second, experienced and knowledgeable staff professionals must be assigned the task of making the new system work. These individuals should be responsible for developing a detailed work plan for implementing the software and then supervising and monitoring its execution. Depending upon the size and complexity of the organization, this may require the full-time concentration of one or more people. They must fully understand both the system's capabilities and how they will be applied within the organization. In addition, although it is time-consuming, individual staff members who will be users should be thoroughly acclimated to the new system. Without such concentrated effort, the hardware may work, and the software may work, but the system as a whole may not: Successful operation of an automated system is totally dependent on knowledgeable people precisely following prescribed policies and procedures.

PHASES OF SYSTEMS IMPROVEMENT

The essential phases of system improvements are planning, evaluation and selection, and implementation.

Developing Planning Documents
Before selecting software, an arts organization must define

its requirements and design a conceptual outline of the system. This document should list the proposed system's basic features and include a description of user information needs, operational processing techniques that will minimize clerical effort, basic hardware requirements (in terms of storage, number of terminals required, etc.), technical software requirements related to the operating systems and software language, and automated linkages to pass information from one system to another automatically as required. Such a document may be likened to an architect's plans—which any knowledgeable builder would require if he is to build to suit the needs of the buyer.

The planning phase is a good time to examine the existing system to see if it can be modified to meet the same design standards indicated in the conceptual outline of the proposed new system. An overall cost estimate for such modification compared against the cost of purchasing a new software package may be needed to help the organization decide which course of action to follow.

Evaluation and Selection

After deciding to purchase software, institutions often must assess which of a variety of software packages will meet their needs. Appropriate available software packages must be identified and each rigorously evaluated by comparing the relative merits and drawbacks of its features to the organization's requirements as specified in the planning documents.

Visiting other similar sites where the software is operational is useful, both to see first-hand how the software performs and to ascertain the vendor's reputation for service and support. Even the vendor's financial condition is a significant concern. Often, the new system will require ongoing maintenance, and if the vendor goes out of business, the arts organization could find itself totally without system support.

Prospective vendors can be identified by referring to software directories and by speaking with knowledgeable individuals at other arts organizations, qualified consultants, and system evaluation services such as DataPro. Vendors should be interviewed, and a request for proposal (RFP) describing explicitly the organization's systems needs should be prepared from the planning documents. These same planning documents will also form the basis of the "evaluation instrument," which the organization will use to compare vendors' responses to the RFP.

Most vendors will present oral and written proposals in a form predefined by the arts organization's evaluators, who will recommend a package after assigning a weighted score to each criterion (e.g., satisfaction of the design and requirements definition, cost, vendor financial stability and relevant experience, and available systems maintenance support). Staff evaluators should verify references, and further, it is often wise for them to make on-site assessments of the software installed at other arts organizations. Systems consultants familiar with arts organizations may be needed to advise the institution about each software package's capabilities and to make recommendations.

Once final selection is made, contracts are prepared and should be rigorously reviewed. Here, too, it is often advisable to seek the assistance of systems consultants.

Implementation

Implementing a software package takes a lot of work. Effective project management and project implementation assistance from the vendor or from systems consultants are often essential.

Project management entails these major elements:
- **Project Planning.** Detailed tasks are defined, responsibilities assigned, and timetables established; project management techniques are used to schedule tasks that may occur in parallel or in sequence;
- **Project Monitoring.** An appropriate project status report-

ing procedure is defined to assist management in determining if individual tasks are performed according to schedule; policy and operational issues that cross organizational lines are identified and resolved;

- **Project Status Review.** An independent, periodic review of the implementation status is conducted to identify problems that require management attention. One of the most frequent problems with new systems is that the completion of certain tasks gets delayed for so long that the starting date is endangered. For an accounting system, the starting date for implementation should be at the beginning of the fiscal year. If that date is in danger of being missed, the organization would normally be advised to wait until the beginning of the next fiscal year. As a result, extra efforts may be needed to complete all of the work required to begin the system's operation on time.

Project Implementation may consist of many discrete elements, including:

- **Current System Features.** The current system should be analyzed to determine functional capabilities;
- **Current System Flow.** The current system flow (i.e., how current transactions are processed) and its relationships with other systems should be analyzed. (For example, an accounting system receives payroll transactions from the payroll system and revenue transactions from a cash receipts system. An understanding of the existing flow and the linkages among systems is essential to installing an automated accounting system, so that the necessary transactions will continue to flow in the new accounting system);
- **Input/Output Documents.** All forms and reports used by the current system should be collected, and each should include a description of its scope, frequency, distribution, and use;
- **Report Requirements.** Formats appropriate to the

capabilities of the software package should be defined, based on discussions with users;

- **Detailed Requirements.** A detailed requirements definition of how the organization will use the new system's capabilities should be prepared;
- **Coding Structure.** The detailed coding structure inherent in the system should be developed to collect, summarize, and report information effectively;
- **Meetings.** Meetings with implementation committees, such as policy and/or steering committees, should be conducted, to resolve operational and policy issues;
- **Base System Testing.** With the vendor, a testing plan should be established for the base system (the standard software package provided by the software vendor);
- **Design Changes.** General and detailed design changes should be made in the proposed system to accommodate automatic interfaces for the passage of data to and from other systems as required;
- **User Manual.** Instruction manuals for user departments should be written to serve as a reference guide to the proposed system;
- **Training Programs.** Training programs should be developed and conducted to introduce staff users to the features of the new system and to acquaint them with their responsibilities in processing transactions into the system;
- **System Conversion Plan.** A conversion plan should be prepared to transfer relevant data from the current system to the proposed system;
- **Final System Testing.** A test should be planned for the final system delivered by the software vendor and assistance in the testing should be provided;
- **Initial Period Consultation.** During the first months after the system goes operational, continued advice and support from the vendor is essential. Problems which often emerge during this period include both those which may

be inherent in the software itself and those which result
from a lack of understanding on the part of staff members
using the system;

- **Post-Implementation Review.** The implemented system
  should be reviewed six to twelve months after it is operational to identify the need for further systems improvements or modifications.

THE ROLE OF THE SOFTWARE VENDOR

Typically, the software vendor assumes full responsibility for
delivering the software package to the institution. The vendor may also be responsible, as set forth in the contract, for
the following:

- Modifying the software to meet the needs of the user;
- Working with the user to reach agreement on systems
  specifications;
- Programming and testing software modifications;
- Installing the software on the user's computer;
- Working with the user during testing and acceptance of
  the software; and
- Providing appropriate documents describing the com-
  puter programs and how the system should be run.

Most often, the software vendor does not provide arts
organizations with sufficient and knowledgeable project
management and project implementation assistance as
described in the previous section. The vendor is usually
responsible for delivering working software and installing
that software on the institution's computer. Because of their
highly concentrated, computer-oriented discipline, software
vendors are not able to devote intense effort to understanding and meeting the individual needs of users. As a result,
this responsibility remains with the arts organization. Frequently, this means that they will require assistance from
other outside professionals experienced in implementing
automated systems.

THE ROLE OF SYSTEMS CONSULTANTS

Systems consultants can assist arts organizations in the difficult task of installing new systems. The scope of their role may include the following:

- Initial systems planning services that involve preparing a conceptual design and requirements definition to serve as a "road map" for systems improvements;
- Assistance in the evaluation and selection of available software to meet organizational needs; and
- Project management and project implementation support at the level of effort required to meet the needs of the arts organization.

A qualified consulting firm should be able to assign experienced consultants who are familiar with the needs of arts organizations. The consultant's role is to assist the staff, who most often have limited time and insufficient experience in the implementation of computer software packages.

A good consultant can be helpful at every step of the automation process, from planning through designing, purchasing, and implementing computer software. Working closely with the staff for a short period of time, a consultant provides a much more economical means of coping with computerization than finding, hiring, and retaining full-time specialized assistance.

Local arts agencies will provide referrals to reputable consultants, or an arts organization might elect to make direct contact with the author of one of the many books which have been written about the subject of office automation.

SUMMARY

Most arts organizations are finding that automated systems have become essential because of increased information processing demands. Fortunately, for the first time, the latest improvements in technology are within the financial reach of almost all organizations.

Before hardware and software are purchased, however, it is important that the organization carefully assess its current operations and develop a reasonable, explicit plan for the new system. Because, in most cases, software can operate only on specific hardware, the software which best meets the organization's needs should be selected first—before choosing the hardware on which it will run.

Once software and hardware have been selected, a rigorous approach to systems implementation should be followed. An implementation plan and systems documentation and training are essential.

Because systems development and implementation are complicated and difficult for those lacking automation experience, arts organizations should seriously consider engaging professional systems consultants to help the staff choose, install, and implement the new system.

Today, many individuals are becoming "computer literate." As such, they are increasingly interested and willing to use the power of computers to support their administrative responsibilities. Computers have proved to provide much opportunity for improved recordkeeping, personnel economy, and efficiency in performing administrative tasks. Perhaps more important, however, is the opportunity to establish an information system that can keep track of the pulse of the arts organization and provide essential information to support management decisionmaking.

C

Financial Statements of
The Henrik Arts Center

EXHIBIT 36
Henrik Arts Center
Statement of Activity

Statement of Activity
Year Ended June 30, 1985
(With comparative totals for 1984)

	Oper- ating Funds	Plant Funds	Endow- ment Funds	Total	Yr. End. 6/30/84 Total
Support & Revenues					
Earned					
Shops	$ 101,000 (H)	—	—	101,000	80,700
Tuition/class fees	48,300 (H)	—	—	48,300	37,800
Admis./tkt. sales	172,000 (H)	—	—	172,000	136,700
Fees/commissions	22,000 (H)	—	—	22,000	17,600
Trips/workshops	14,400 (H)	—	—	14,400	10,900
Investment	176,500 (H)	—	—	176,500	178,400
Other income	21,000 (H)	—	—	21,000	19,400
Total Earned	555,200	—	—	555,200	481,500
Grants					
City	15,000 (H)	—	—	15,000	33,500
County	110,000 (H)	—	—	110,000	100,400
State	75,600 (H)	—	—	75,600	67,000
Federal	45,800 (H)	—	—	45,800	113,600
Private	34,200 (H)	—	—	34,200	25,500
Total Grants	280,600	—	—	280,600	340,000
Contributions					
Individs.—Annual	215,000 (H)	—	—	215,000	195,600
Corps./Fndns.	720,000 (H)	—	—	720,000	650,000
Memberships	47,200 (H)	—	—	47,200	35,200
Total Contributions	982,200	—	—	982,200	880,800
Total Support and Revenue	$1,818,000 (G)	—	—	1,818,000	1,702,300 (G)

The letter designations above refer to the accumulations used to calculate the ratios illustrated in Chapter 8, where:

(D)=Total Expenses
For 1984   (D)=(S)−(T)
$1,727,000=$1,778,000−$51,000*
*(T)=Depreciation for 1984 is not noted on the statement and has been given to the reader for comparability to 1985.

(F)=Total Support and Revenue
For 1984   (F)=(G)−(T)
($24,700)=($75,700)−($51,000)

(I)=Program Expense Categories
For 1984   (I)=(S)−(T)
Curatorial $151,700=156,300−4,600
Conservation   124,400=144,000−19,600
Exhibitions   357,000=357,000−0
Crafts Council   72,100=84,800−12,700
Publicity and pub. rel.   47,100=51,000−3,900
Fundraising   41,000=49,800−8,800
Div. Administration   66,100=67,500−1,400

EXHIBIT 36
Continued

	Oper-ating Funds	Plant Funds	Endow-ment Funds	Total	Yr. End. 6/30/84 Total
Expenses					
Museum Division					
Primary Programs					
Curatorial	$192,000 (I)	4,100	—	196,100	156,300 (S)
Conservation	131,100 (I)	19,200	—	150,300	144,000 (S)
Exhibitions	390,100 (I)	—	—	390,100	357,000 (S)
Crafts Council	87,000 (I)	12,500	—	99,500	84,800 (S)
Support programs					
Publicity and pub. rel.	57,000 (I)	3,800	—	60,800	51,000 (S)
Fundraising	47,000 (I)	8,200	—	55,200	49,800 (S)
Div. administration	70,400 (I)	1,300	—	71,700	67,500 (S)
Total Museum Div.	974,600	49,100	—	1,023,700	910,400
Ballet Division . . .	. . .	. . .		. . .	. . .
Education Division . . .	. . .	. . .	. . .	. . .	. . .
Total Expenses	1,946,000 (D)	49,100	—	1,995,100	1,778,000 (S)
Excess (deficiency) of support and revenue over expenses before capital additions	(128,000) (F)	(49,100)	—	(177,100)	(75,700) (G)
Capital additions					
Gifts and grants	—	25,600	75,000	100,600	60,000
Net investment income	—	—	5,500	5,500	2,100
Net realized investment gains (losses)	—	—	(12,000)	(12,000)	4,500
Total	—	25,600	68,500	94,100	66,600
Excess (deficiency) of support and revenue over expenses after capital additions	(128,000)	(23,500)	68,500	(83,000)	(9,100)
Fund balances, beginning of period	507,000	5,270,100	2,831,500	8,608,600	8,617,700
Add (deduct) transfers	(53,400)	53,400	—	—	
Fund balances, end of period	$325,600	5,300,000	2,900,000	8,525,600	8,608,600

EXHIBIT 37
Henrik Arts Center
Balance Sheet

HENRIK ARTS CENTER
Balance Sheet
June 30, 1985
(With comparative totals for 1984)

	Oper-ating Funds	Plant Funds	Endow-ment Funds	Total	6/30/84 Total
Assets					
Current Assets					
Cash	$ 22,500	—	—	22,500	153,500
Receivables less reserve of $8,500	106,000	—	—	106,000	48,000
Investments	55,000	—	—	55,000	238,000
Inventories at lower of cost (FIFO) or market	62,000	—	—	62,000	85,000
Total Current Assets	245,500	—	—	245,500	524,500 (M)
Fixed Assets, net of depreciation	—	5,300,000	—	5,300,000	5,270,100
Art Collection	—	—	—	—	—
Investments	400,000	—	2,900,000	3,300,000	3,200,000 (N)
Total Assets	$645,500 (A)	5,300,000	2,900,000	8,845,500	8,994,600

The letter designations above refer to the accumulations used to calculate the ratios illustrated in Chapter 8, where:

(A)=Expendable Assets
For 1984   (A)=(M)+(N−O)
$893,000=
  $524,500+($3,200,000−$2,831,500)

(B)=Total Liabilities

(C)=Expendable Fund Balances
For 1984   (C)=(P)+(Q)+(R)
$507,000=$320,000+$104,000+$83,000

(E)=Nonexpendable Fund Balances
For 1984   (E)=(O)

EXHIBIT 37
Continued

	Oper- ating Funds	Plant Funds	Endow- ment Funds	Total	6/30/84 Total
Liabilities and Fund Balances					
Current Liabilities					
Accounts payable and accrual expenses	$ 86,000			86,000	118,000
Deferred revenue and restricted gifts, current portion	150,000			150,000	170,000
Total current liabilities	236,000 (B)			236,000	288,000 (B)
Deferred revenue and restricted gifts, non- current portion	83,900 (B)			83,900	98,000 (B)
Fund balances					
Endowment			2,900,000 (E)	2,900,000	2,831,500 (O)
Land, buildings and equipment		5,300,000		5,300,000	5,270,100
Unrestricted					
Designated for investment	250,000			250,000	320,000 (P)
Designated for plant expansion	50,000			50,000	104,000 (Q)
Unappropriated	25,600			25,600	83,000 (R)
Total fund balances	325,600 (C)	5,300,000	2,900,000	8,525,600	8,608,600
Total liabilities and fund balances	$645,500	5,300,000	2,900,000	8,845,500	8,994,600

About the American Council for the Arts

The American Council for the Arts (ACA) addresses significant issues in the arts by promoting communications, management improvement, and problem-solving among those who shape and implement arts policy. ACA currently accomplishes this by:

- fostering communication and cooperation among arts groups and leaders in the public and private sectors;
- promoting advocacy on behalf of *all* the arts;
- sponsoring research, analysis, studies;
- publishing books, manuals, *Vantage Point* magazine and ACA *Update* for leaders and managers in the arts;
- providing information and clearinghouse services;
- providing technical assistance to arts managers and administrators.

Board of Directors

Chairman of the Board
Marshall S. Cogan
President
Milton Rhodes
Vice Chairmen
Eugene Dorsey
Mary Shands
Esther Wachtell
Homer C. Wadsworth
Chairman,
Executive Committee
Louis Harris
Secretary
John Kilpatrick
Treasurer
Sam F. Segnar

Neale M. Albert
Jane Alexander
Ben Barkin
Anne Bartley
Theodore Bikel
Edward M. Block
John Brademas
Elliot R. Cattarulla
Mrs. George P. Caulkins, Jr.
Donald Conrad
Mrs. Catherine G. Curran
Barbaralee Diamonstein-
    Spielvogel
Peter Duchin
Mrs. Robert Fowler
Arthur Gelber, O.C.
Jack Golodner
Louis T. Hagopian
Linda Hoeschler
Richard Hunt
Lane Kirkland
Mrs. Fred Lazarus III
Robert Leys

James M. McClymond
Michael Newton
Alwin Nikolais
Murray Charles Pfister
David Rockefeller, Jr.
Henry C. Rogers
Rodney Rood
Terry T. Saario
Robert Sakowitz
Daniel I. Sargent
Frank Saunders
Edward Saxe
Stephen Stamas
Roselyne Swig
Mrs. Gerald Westby
Charles Yates

Executive Director
William Keens
Special Counsel
for National Policy
Jack G. Duncan

Major Contributors to the American Council for the Arts

At press time, special thanks are extended to the following for their contributions in support of ACA's operations, programs, and special projects.

BENEFACTORS ($20,000 and up)

Aetna Life & Casualty Foundation•American Telephone & Telegraph Company
Atlantic Richfield Company•Edward M. Block•CBS Incorporated•Marshall S. Cogan
Exxon Corporation•Gannett Foundation•InterNorth Foundation•Knoll International
Louis Harris & Associates•National Endowment for the Arts•Philip Morris Incorporated

---

SUSTAINERS ($10,000–$19,999)

NW Ayer Inc.•Collier Graphic Services•Dayton Hudson Corporation
Barbaralee Diamonstein-Spielvogel•Equitable Life Assurance Society
New York State Council on the Arts•Murray Charles Pfister•Progressive Corporation
Rockefeller Foundation•Rev. & Mrs. Alfred Shands III•Sterling Regal Inc.

PATRONS ($5,000–$9,999)

The Allstate Foundation•American Stock Exchange•BATUS Inc.
Chesebrough-Pond's Inc.•The Chevron Fund•General Electric Foundation
IBM Corporation•ITT•John Kilpatrick, Jr.•Knight Foundation•Loral Corporation
Mobil Foundation, Inc.•Tom Newman•Peat, Marwick, Mitchell & Co.
Phillips Petroleum Foundation•R.J. Reynolds Industries, Inc.•Sakowitz, Inc.
Shell Companies Foundation•Standard Oil Company (Ohio)•Mr. & Mrs. Richard L. Swig
Warner Communications Inc.•Mrs. Gerald H. Westby•Xerox Corporation

---

DONORS ($2,000–$4,999)

Actual Art Foundation•Allied Corporation•American Airlines, Inc.
Avon Products Foundation, Inc.•Bankers Trust Company•Livio Borghese
Bristol-Myers Fund•Chemical Bank•Donald G. Conrad•Cooper Industries
Dart & Kraft, Inc.•Marion V. Day•Emerson Electric Company
Esmark, Inc. Foundation•Estee Lauder Companies•Federated Department Stores, Inc.
Ford Motor Company Fund•Hanes Companies, Inc.•Heublein Foundation, Inc.
Horan Engraving•Lazard Freres & Company•Monsanto Fund
NL Industries Foundation, Inc.•J.C. Penney Company, Inc.•Procter & Gamble Fund
Prudential Insurance Company Foundation•Raytheon Company
Reader's Digest Association, Inc.•Robert Sakowitz•Daniel I. Sargent
Union Pacific Foundation•U.S. Steel Foundation•Western Electric Fund
Westinghouse Electric Fund

CONTRIBUTORS ($1,000–$1,999)

American Broadcasting Companies, Inc.•American Express•Fundacion Angel Ramos
Atelier Royce Ltd.•Anne Bartley•Ben Barkin•Bechtel Foundation•Robert Bernhard
Binney & Smith•Bozell & Jacobs, Inc.•Carter Hawley Hale Stores, Inc.
Mrs. George Caulkins•Chase Manhattan Bank•Cigna Corporation
Coca-Cola Company•Conoco, Inc.•Mr. & Mrs. Earle M. Craig, Jr.
Mrs. Catherine G. Curran•Ethyl Corporation•Arthur Gelber
General Dynamics Corporation•General Mills, Inc.•Toni K. Goodale
Mrs. John D. Gordon•Gulf + Western Foundation•Hartmarx Corporation
H.J. Heinz Company Foundation•Mr. & Mrs. John G. Hoeschler•Hercules, Inc.
Knight-Ridder Newspapers, Inc.•Levi Strauss Foundation•Arthur Levitt Jr.
The Manhattan Life Insurance Company•Manufacturers Hanover Trust
James M. McClymond•Metropolitan Life Foundation•Monsanto Fund
National Computer Systems•New York Life Foundation
New York Times Company Foundation
Olsen Gallery•PepsiCo Foundation•Pfizer Foundation, Inc.
Pogo Producing Company•David Rockefeller, Jr.
Henry C. Rogers•Rubbermaid Incorporated•Frank A. Saunders
Schering-Plough Foundation, Inc.•Scurlock Oil Company
Sears, Roebuck & Company•Sam F. Segnar•Serra di Felice Gallery
Textron, Inc.•Times-Mirror Company•Touche Ross & Co.
Esther Wachtell•Lawrence A. Wein